Like the Lightning

Like the Lightning

The Dynamics of the Ignatian Exercises

David L. Fleming, SJ

The Son of Man in his day will be like the lightning that flashes from one end of the sky to the other.

Lk 17:24

SAINT LOUIS
THE INSTITUTE OF JESUIT SOURCES

Series III: Original Studies Composed in English

Number 21: Like the Lightning: The Dynamics of the Ignatian Exercises

©2004 The Institute of Jesuit Sources
3601 Lindell Boulevard
Saint Louis, MO 63108
TEL: 314-977-7257
FAX: 314-977-7263
e-mail: IJS@SLU.EDU
Website: www.jesuitsources.com

Library of Congress Control Number: 2004113267
ISBN 1-880810-58-1

First printing 2004

CONTENTS

Introduction

AN EXPLANATION

"What kind of a book about the *Spiritual Exercises* of St. Ignatius are you writing?"

That was the question that first greeted my admission that I was taking time off from teaching to write a book on the Exercises. In this introduction, then, I want to be helpful by explaining what I intend to do and what my hopes and desires are for this kind of comment on the Exercises.

When I first wrote *A Contemporary Reading of the Spiritual Exercises of St. Ignatius*, the subtitle was *A Companion to St. Ignatius's Text* and my text was identified as an experimental edition.[1] In 1978 the first of the double-text editions was published, a literal translation of Ignatius's Spanish Autograph text facing my own contemporary reading.[2] Many readers questioned whether I was making another translation or trying to paraphrase loosely the classic Ignatian text, *Ejercicios Espirituales*. In response to their inquiry, I focused on my use of the word *reading*. I explained that I was attempting to present to a contemporary English language reader a way of accessing the Ignatian text so that this person could exclaim, "Oh, that is what he [Ignatius] is saying."

We commonly ask a person to *say* what he or she really means. Perhaps what the person has said is obscure in its language or perhaps the thought

---

[1] David Fleming, SJ, *A Contemporary Reading of the Spiritual Exercises of St. Ignatius: A Companion to St. Ignatius's Text* (St. Louis: Institute of Jesuit Sources, 1976). This text was also published as *Modern Spiritual Exercises: A Contemporary Reading of the Spiritual Exercises of St. Ignatius* (Garden City, N.Y.: Image Books, 1983).

[2] This later book is titled *Draw Me into Your Friendship: A Literal Translation and a Contemporary Reading of the Spiritual Exercises* (St. Louis: Institute of Jesuit Sources, 1996). The first double-text edition was simply titled *The Spiritual Exercises of Saint Ignatius: A Literal Translation and a Contemporary Reading* (St. Louis: Institute of Jesuit Sources, 1978). There was a slightly revised text published in 1980, and the four reprintings (1982, 1985, 1989, and 1991) were of that revised text.

process is tangled. Maybe we are people who just need a simple uncluttered explanation. Without trying for a more accurate translation of the Ignatian Spanish text, and without attempting to rewrite his *Spiritual Exercises* in my own way, I wanted in *A Contemporary Reading* to let Ignatius speak as clearly as he could so that we could better understand him today. I believed that, by first letting Ignatius help us enter into his dynamic movement and thought expression, we could then return to his literal text with a kind of "aha!" understanding. If I presented a way for all of us to read the text with greater insight and clarity, then the stark and sometimes difficult language of Ignatius would no longer stand as a block to the easy flow of the retreat.

If it was difficult then for me to explain what I intended to do in my presentation of a "reading" of the text, I fear that this present book will also suffer from a certain obscurity of purpose. I do not intend to write a commentary on the Exercises, such as the excellent and thorough *Understanding the Spiritual Exercises* by Michael Ivens, SJ.[3] I am not writing a "how to" book, which would outline a retreat to be made in eight days or in thirty days or, in the everyday-life retreat, over a period of months; examples of such are *Choosing Christ in the World* and *Lightworks*, both by Joseph A. Tetlow, SJ.[4]

---

[3] Michael Ivens, SJ, *Understanding the Spiritual Exercises* (Leominster, U.K.: Gracewing, 1998). Besides his recent commentary, other popular ones have been William A. Barry, SJ, *Letting God Come Close: An Approach to the Ignatian Spiritual Exercises* (Chicago: Loyola Press, 2002); Katherine Dyckman, SNJM, Mary Garvin, SNJM, and Elizabeth Liebert, SNJM, *The Spiritual Exercises Reclaimed: Uncovering Liberating Possibilities for Women* (Mahwah, N.J.: Paulist Press, 2001); and Joseph A. Tetlow, SJ, *Ignatius Loyola. Spiritual Exercises* (New York: Crossroad, 1996). Older, well-known commentaries are Hervé Coathalem, SJ, *Ignatian Insights: A Guide to the Complete Spiritual Exercises* (Taichung, Taiwan: Kuangchi Press, 1961); Gilles Cusson, SJ, *Biblical Theology and the Spiritual Exercises* (St. Louis: Institute of Jesuit Sources, 1988); and William A. M. Peters, SJ, *The Spiritual Exercises of St. Ignatius: Exposition and Interpretation* (Rome: Centrum Ignatianum Spiritualitatis, 1978).

[4] Joseph A. Tetlow, SJ, *Choosing Christ in the World: A Handbook for Directing the Spiritual Exercises of St. Ignatius Loyola According to Annotations Eighteen and Nineteen* (rev. ed., St. Louis: Institute of Jesuit Sources, 1999); this edition includes as an appendix the author's separately published *Lightworks: Some Simple Exercises According to Annotation Eighteen of the Spiritual Exercises* (St. Louis: Institute of Jesuit Sources, 1999). In addition to Tetlow's works, practical helps in giving the Exercises are found in Marian Cowan, CSJ, and John Futrell, SJ,

I hope rather to reflect on the Exercises as a unit, in their integral makeup and in their overall movement. Beyond offering a "reading" of the text, I am now trying to shed light on the interrelationship of the many elements that are the engines of the Ignatian dynamics or movement. It is my intention to highlight some aspects of the Exercises in such a way that the reader might gain a freshness of insight with which to direct an Ignatian retreat from a new depth of understanding or to find the making of a retreat a vastly richer experience of the dynamics of God's activity.

Key to the Ignatian Exercises is our living and working with God. God—our Trinitarian God—is the source of all life, and God it is who is bringing about the Kingdom. Ignatius images well this Trinitarian God in his Incarnation contemplation [101] – [109]. Throughout the course of the Exercises, we keep seeing God and Jesus like lightning flashes that illuminate a whole scene, be it ever so briefly. And then there is another flash, and again we see clearly, if only for a short time. The Exercises bring home to us the meaning of the Scripture quote: "The Son of Man in his day will be like lightning that flashes from one end of the sky to the other" (Lk 17:24). The Exercises evoke in us the flashes of lightning: God and Jesus shine out into our life and into our world, and we see as we have not seen before. The lightning flashes reveal various faces of God that, being new to us, draw forth from us new ways of relating to God. Like the lightning, the Exercises help us to experience through many bright flashes a God who embraces us in an ever more transparent relationship. Simply said, the Spiritual Exercises facilitate our growth in the spiritual life as we come to know and to respond to God who shows his face to us in everyday life.

Companions in Grace: A Handbook for Directors of the Spiritual Exercises of St. Ignatius of Loyola (St. Louis: Institute of Jesuit Sources, 2000); Gilles Cusson, SJ, *The Spiritual Exercises Made in Everyday Life: A Method and a Biblical Interpretation* (St. Louis: Institute of Jesuit Sources, 1989); John English, SJ, *Spiritual Freedom: From an Experience of the Ignatian Exercises to the Art of Spiritual Guidance* (Chicago: Loyola Press, Second Edition, 1995); Tom O'Hara, *At Home with the Spirit: A Retreat in Daily Life* (Mahwah, N.J.: Paulist Press, 1992); Martin E. Palmer, SJ, *On Giving the Spiritual Exercises: The Early Jesuit Manuscript Directories and the Official Directory of 1599* (St. Louis: Institute of Jesuit Sources, 1996); Carol Ann Smith, SHCJ, and Eugene Merz, SJ, *Moment by Moment: A Retreat in Everyday Life* (Notre Dame: Ave Maria Press, 2000); and John A. Veltri, SJ, *Orientations,* Vol. 1: *A Collection of Helps for Prayer:* Vol. II: *Annotation 19* (Guelph: Loyola Press, 2000).

There are three major divisions in my book. In the first part I intend to show the dynamics writ large as we consider some of the major elements and themes that make up the flow of the Exercises. Because I am examining the whole of the Exercises through the lenses of those different elements or themes, I know that we are looking, as it were, at the same terrain but through different templates. This approach results in seemingly repetitious observations, but I hope that the complexity of the dynamics involved is thus clearly revealed. In the second part, I zero in on particular exercises that shape the dynamic flow, and again I make no excuses if the reader feels that "this seems familiar." The Exercises' dynamics are not only writ large; they are also writ finely, in the discreet movements of the individual exercises. Finally, in the third part, I touch lightly on discernment and the Ignatian guidelines (so-called rules) for discernment in terms of their sense of movement, and not so much in terms of analysis or historical explanation. I have added, in the appendix, a summary or review essay which considers the Exercises in terms of their movement or dynamics.

Of course, I admit that I meet Ignatius Loyola in my own experience of living as an American Jesuit of the twenty-first century. I love and respect what he has to say, and throughout my many years of living Jesuit life, I have listened carefully to him speak through his *Spiritual Exercises*, his *Autobiography*, and his *Constitutions of the Society of Jesus*. I feel that Ignatius and I have lived, together, by God's grace, the experiences he has shared in all these documents. Like any close friend, I think I know what Ignatius means by this or that expression, example, or direction.

Similarly, Ignatius has had many other friends over the past four centuries who claim that same kind of confidential understanding. We, now living in the twenty-first century, have profited greatly from the writings, talks, retreats, and directions that these friends of Ignatius, both women and men, have shared with us since the lifetime of Ignatius up till the present day. In all friendships, no one friend is truly the alter ego, so divinely enhanced is each one's uniqueness. But good friends continue to help give ways of understanding their friend, namely, Ignatius Loyola, to others, even after centuries of such revelations have passed. In our own day, Father Pedro Arrupe, SJ, former superior general of the Jesuits, has served in a very special way as one such friend of Ignatius for me and for many others. I will always be grateful for his stimulus to our contemporary study of Ignatian spirituality.

I am reflecting out of my more than thirty years' experiences of teaching university theology courses on the Spiritual Exercises, giving numerous workshops and conferences, and then conducting thirty-day retreats for members of the Institute of Religious Formation (1971-1976), members of the Focus on Leadership program (1976-1979), and Jesuits in their tertianship program (1976-1979, and 1999-2000). As I write this book, I am presuming that the reader has some familiarity with the Ignatian text and, I am hoping, an experience of the full Exercises as well. It is helpful to have the text of the Exercises readily at hand while reading this book. I would suggest my own text since it includes the literal translation by Elder Mullan, which closely follows the Spanish Autograph text. The respective text translations by George E. Ganss, SJ, by Louis J. Puhl, SJ, and by Joseph A. Tetlow, SJ, are also helpful and easily available.[5] To have experienced Ignatian retreats (in their fullness and in their shorter forms) and to have the Ignatian text at hand, then, are desirable conditions for entering into the approach I take in this book.

I will be pleased if some readers find me friend enough of Ignatius that I can somehow help them, be they longtime friends or relatively new acquaintances, to appreciate ever better the graced instrument of the Spiritual Exercises which Ignatius has shared with us in the church. I am especially happy to dedicate this book to my Jesuit brothers, all of them with me, Ignatius's companions and "friends in the Lord."

I am grateful to Father John Padberg, SJ, director of the Institute of Jesuit Sources, and to Father Ralph Renner, SJ, editor *par excellence*, to Father Philip Fischer, SJ, and to the late Father William Stauder, SJ, for their interest, critique, and encouragement through all the stages of bringing this book to publication.

David L. Fleming, SJ

---

[5] George E. Ganss, SJ, *The Spiritual Exercises of Saint Ignatius: A Translation and Commentary* (St. Louis: Institute of Jesuit Sources, 1992); Louis J. Puhl, SJ, *The Spiritual Exercises of St. Ignatius: A New Translation Based on Studies in the Language of the Autograph* (Chicago: Loyola Press, 1968); Joseph A. Tetlow, SJ, *Ignatius Loyola: Spiritual Exercises* (New York: Crossroad, 1996).

PART I

LIGHTNING FLASHES

Chapter One

WHAT KIND OF BOOK IS *SPIRITUAL EXERCISES*?[1]

The book *Spiritual Exercises* (original Spanish, *Ejercicios Espirituales*) by Ignatius Loyola has been in print for some 450 years and has been translated into most of the world's major languages. What is odd about *Spiritual Exercises* is that, although it is a book, we cannot pick it up and read it in the way that we ordinarily approach a book.

Those of us familiar with the Ignatian text tend to take for granted the title of the book and thereby fail to realize all its implications. The book is what its very title proclaims—an exercise book. Realizing it is a book of exercises can significantly affect our understanding and expectation of an Ignatian retreat. If we have had any experience with an exercise book for learning math or English grammar in our primary school days, we know that we also had to have a text book, which was central to learning the class matter, for the role of the accompanying exercise book was to call forth an active use of the material presented in the content book.

Not for Reading

In a similar way, Ignatius wrote a book of spiritual exercises. As with any exercise book, the one who uses it has to have another source for the content, that is, the subject matter to be exercised. For Ignatius, the content matter to be used for his *Spiritual Exercises* is primarily our own life experiences as seen in the light of the life experiences of Jesus depicted in the Gospels. His exercise book helps us enter into an active use of our life's content in its relation with God and with the Jesus of the Gospels.

---

[1] A version of this introduction was published in the Indian journal of spirituality *Ignis* under the title "What Are the Spiritual Exercises?" (27, no. 1 [1998]: 43-47) and also in the Jesuits of the Missouri Province publication *Jesuit Bulletin* in two parts, "What Are the Spiritual Exercises?" (76, no. 1 [Spring 1997]: 12-13) and "Invited into a World Charged with Grandeur" (76, no. 2 [Fall 1997]: 12-13).

In 1522 Ignatius began putting his little book together from the notes that he himself made as he reflected on his experiences of how God seemed to be leading him in his life. In the midst of his transition from a worldly-minded *caballero* to a knight in the service of God, Ignatius spent eleven months in a little town in Spain called Manresa, where he prayed and struggled with God. He described his experiences as similar to that of a teacher educating a schoolboy, with God as the teacher and himself as the schoolboy. It was during this reflective time in Manresa that Ignatius had some of his most illuminative mystical experiences. Although years later he related some of these experiences in a book often called his *Autobiography*,[2] there are no explicit references to mysticism to be found in his more famous book *Spiritual Exercises*. Rather, the influence of these mystical experiences at Manresa is to be seen in the way he wrote down those exercises, an experience-based presentation that would allow us coming after him to explore and grow in our own experience of our relationship with God and awareness of God calling and leading us throughout our life.

Through his conversations with others, Ignatius discovered early on that the notes which he had made about his own experiences had proved to be helpful to them. As he kept working with men and women desiring to grow in a relationship with God, he would nuance, correct, or add to his own notes.

---

[2] Ignatius Loyola reluctantly agreed to dictate his life story to a fellow Jesuit, Luís Gonçalves da Câmara. Ignatius did not want da Câmara to take notes during the sharing of his story. Since da Câmara a was blessed with a retentive memory, he would run back to his room, make notes of what he had heard, and then later write or dictate the full text. As a result, the book is peculiar in being identified as an "autobiography." The book covers the time period from Ignatius's conversion to his arrival in Rome (1521-1538).

Common English translations are Parmananda Divarkar, SJ, trans., *A Pilgrim's Testament: The Memoirs of Saint Ignatius of Loyola* (St. Louis: Institute of Jesuit Sources, 1995); John F. O'Callaghan, SJ, trans., with John C. Olin, ed., *The Autobiography of Saint Ignatius Loyola with Related Documents* (New York: Harper and Row, 1974); Joseph N. Tylenda, SJ, trans., *The Pilgrim's Journey: The Autobiography of Ignatius of Loyola* (Wilmington, Del.: Michael Glazier, 1985); William Yeomans, SJ, trans., *Inigo Text: Original Testament* (Inigo Enterprise, 1989); William J. Young, SJ, trans, *St. Ignatius's Own Story as Told to Luis González de Cámera* [Spanish form of the Portuguese name Luís Gonçalves da Câmara] (Chicago: Loyola U. Press, 1968).

Always Adapting

Gradually—after some twenty-five years—these notes evolved into the published book *Spiritual Exercises*. When the book was printed in 1548, tradition has it that Ignatius kept all five hundred copies. He would present the book only to someone who had already gone through the prayer experiences of his Spiritual Exercises, most often directed by Ignatius himself. This person, who was now moving from being retreatant to being director, was entrusted by Ignatius with the *Spiritual Exercises* book. Ignatius's concern was that the person who was going to give these Exercises to another would have a sense of how to adapt them and so apply them to that individual. Just as the book cannot simply be read, so also it is presumed by Ignatius that this book is special in that it cannot be helpfully adapted to another individual except by a person who has truly had the experience of making the Exercises.

This notion of adaptation is reinforced by the fact that the book does not start with a "Chapter One." It begins with a series of "helps" (the Spanish *anotaciones*, translated literally as "annotations") for the one who is going to be using the book in directing another. The "helps" are all given as hints or reminders about adapting and applying the Exercises inasmuch as God works with each individual in a unique way. Even though the director using the book has already profited from the experience of the Exercises, Ignatius was concerned that this new director might think about a retreatant: "God has worked with me in this way; therefore God must work with you in the same way." But it is an Ignatian principle that God works intimately with each one of us. Consequently, the whole structure of this book is always to be seen in terms of adaptation. We will consider further this aspect of the Exercises in chapter 4.

Facilitating Relationships

Ignatius envisioned his printed book as only a help in an active three-way conversation. Commonly today we use the terms "retreat director" and "retreatant." Ignatius never used substantive nouns for these persons; instead, he used active phrases, like "the one who gives the Exercises" and "the one who receives or makes the Exercises." His stress was evidently on the activity of the relationship involved in a retreat based on his book *Spiritual Exercises*. For Ignatius, the activity of the one giving the Exercises and the one making the Exercises, had to be related, above all, to the activity of God, who is *the* Director of the retreat experience. The Exercises, then, always involve a three-way conversation. The book *Spiritual Exercises* was meant to be itself a help in facilitating this conversation between the retreatant and God, between the director and God, and between the retreatant and the director.

Many Kinds of Exercises

What kind of exercises are we talking about? In his first notation at the beginning of the book, Ignatius says that, just as there are many different kinds of physical exercises, so too there are many different kinds of spiritual exercises. Some commonly used spiritual exercises are saying the rosary, participating at Mass, spiritual reading, and perhaps having a spiritual conversation with someone. God can enter into our daily living through many kinds of activities, and so we might identify them for ourselves as *spiritual.* Perhaps listening to certain kinds of music, walking in a forest or along an ocean beach, or watching a baby playing in its crib can become the "exercise" in which God touches each of us. There are specific prayer exercises identified in a Spiritual Exercises retreat, but we need also to take in and reflect on all the activities of our retreat day if we are to realize how God and we may be interacting through the whole movement of the retreat.

Looking towards Growth

What is the purpose of the *Spiritual Exercises* book? Ignatius has provided those of us in the Catholic tradition with a method or help in a conversion process. Ignatius never uses the word *conversion,* even though the roots of his Exercises are found in such a dramatic change in his own life direction and his newfound relation with God. Conversion is a change of attitude, a change of heart; it can indicate a change from a life of sin to a life of virtue, but it can just as well mean a change from a good life to an even more zealous life. God continues to call each of us throughout our lifetime to a growth we call *conversion.* The Exercises are meant to facilitate this process.

Retreat Length

Although there are Ignatian retreats of various lengths such as three days and five days and eight days, why did Ignatius identify thirty days for the full experience of the Exercises? From the time of the book's publication, Ignatius was questioned about his choice of thirty days. Some church officials pointed out that forty days as in Lent, fifty day as in the Pentecost season, nine days as in novenas were common numbers in the Christian tradition; thirty days seems to have no precedent. Ignatius is said to have replied simply, "I have dealt with a lot of people, and it works." For over 450 years, the thirty-day retreat experience has been effective in countless lives in the Christian community. As Ignatius concluded from his own experience, the Spiritual Exercises "work" in a time period of some thirty days. We should note that Ignatius also identified the accommodation of this thirty-day experience to a retreat model spread out over a longer period of a person's everyday-life activities for those who could not free themselves up for the concentrated thirty-day experience. But, whatever the length of the accommodated retreat, always at its origin is the basic thirty-day experience.

The Ones Who Exercise

The major group of people for whom Ignatius wrote the book *Spiritual Exercises* is the people who want to come to a decision about the direction of their life. Do I want to get married—and to whom—and where is God's lead? Do I want to stay single—and where is God's lead? Do I want to become a religious or a priest—and where is God's lead? Do I want to spend my life in church service in a foreign county—and where is God's lead? Perhaps the decision is more about a lifestyle than a life choice. Do I choose to live a simple lifestyle—and what is God's lead? Do I want to align myself more with a communal life—and what is God's lead? Ignatius also had in mind people who wanted to reform their lives or make some changes in the way of life that they were living. They, too, find themselves touched with their need for God and directed in their choice through the methodology of the Exercises.

A common experience today for a growing number of people is to make the Spiritual Exercises retreat within the context of their everyday life and commitments. Many people cannot take thirty days off and go to a retreat house or a desert experience. In his own day Ignatius knew that many people had jobs and responsibilities and so could little afford the time or expense for the full thirty-day experience away. Within the series of helps that begin the book, Ignatius notes that there are various ways of making the Exercises, even in their entirety. He suggests, then, the possibility of extending the retreat over some months, perhaps even a year. Such a retreat would proceed in the orderly method which Ignatius outlines, with an hour or so given to formal prayer every day. A meeting with the one giving the Exercises might occur every week, instead of the everyday expectation of the concentrated thirty-day experience.

Always More

What is the end result of making the Spiritual Exercises? Does the book *Spiritual Exercises* have an ending? Neither the retreat experience nor the book has a conclusion. We must remember that our basic image is exercise. Should we ever stop exercising physically or spiritually? After making the Spiritual Exercises, one can say: "I have reached a certain point in my life's journey, and I have a sense that this is the direction that God would continue to have me go. I feel encouraged and strengthened in my journeying with God." Ignatius intends that we experience God being actively present and actively laboring in life and in creation. He also helps us to realize our readiness to respond to God and to God's invitation to labor with Christ "for the greater glory of God."

Ignatius wants us to live in a world filled with God's love; he wants us to be extensions of God's love in our everyday world. Ignatius invites us through the Spiritual Exercises into an experience of that same vision that he had—a world charged with the grandeur of God. Through the Exercises, we enter into the dynamics of playing our part with Jesus in bringing about the reign of God.

Chapter Two

THE DYNAMICS OF THE EXERCISES

Once we see that the book *Spiritual Exercises* needs to be understood as a true exercise book, then it comes as no surprise that the parts of this book do not necessarily follow in a logical or chronological order. For example, the emphasis is not on the chronology of Jesus' life, though we might be inclined to surmise this from the flow of the Second, Third, and Fourth Weeks.

In fact, Ignatius does not follow the chronology of Jesus' life found in any one Gospel. Given the stage of Scripture studies in his day, Ignatius cannot be faulted in his choices of Gospel mysteries from all four Gospels for violating what we today see as the integrity of each Gospel. As a typically fundamentalist renaissance man, Ignatius would not have been aware that each Gospel has its own point of view, its own structure, and its own theology.[1] For Ignatius, the Gospels present salvation history; *this* is the kind of history that he asks us to recall in the prelude before each contemplation. Since he was ignorant of the twentieth century's "new approach" to Gospel study, Ignatius's choices of Gospel mysteries from the four Gospels were indiscriminate because the chronology of events in any one of the Gospels—which he may or may not have been aware of—has little importance in his judgment.[2] For Ignatius (being unknowingly a good

---

[1] "We are not doing justice to the gospels when we take bits and pieces from the four of them. Each gospel has its own point of view, its own structure, its own theology" (William J. Dalton, SJ, "How To Use the Bible in the Exercises," in *The Word of God in the Spiritual Exercises* [Rome: Centrum Ignatianum Spiritualitatis, 1979], 11).

[2] David M. Stanley, SJ, expresses a different view: "There is a certain manifest Ludolphian residue in Ignatius's presentation of The Mysteries of the Life of Our Lord, and elsewhere in the Exercises, which (I make bold to assert) should be ignored nowadays by the director and, indeed, by the exercitant. I mention only three examples for the sake of brevity: the legendary accretions with which medieval piety delighted to surround the sacred text, the age-old tendency—going back to Tatian — of 'harmonizing' the disparate, sometimes contradictory account in the Gospels, finally (and this is less serious) the occasional re-aligning of the sequence of events

evangelist), the timeline of events is not the main path to our coming to know Jesus. What Ignatius calls *mysteries* refers to the incidents in the gospel accounts that sum up a particular story. The medieval *mystery plays* caught the same meaning, and this meaning continues in our use of the *mysteries* of the rosary. For Ignatius, who in his directions has each retreatant enter into his or her own gospel story line, the mysteries of the Gospels are chosen to fit the flow of the retreat, not according to a chronology peculiar to any one Gospel.

When we are engaged in familiar physical exercises, there is a flow in our movements—what we might call their *dynamics*. So, too, if we are exercising well spiritually, there is a flow or dynamic movement which takes precedence over a logical or chronological ordering. Ignatius seems concerned about this *flow* of the Exercises, as we can see from his directions for the daily conversations between the retreatant and the director.

Describing Dynamics

"The dynamics of the Spiritual Exercises" is an often-used phrase. The obvious question is: What do we mean by the word *dynamics* when we speak of the Spiritual Exercises?

Webster's dictionary gives as the first meaning for the word *dynamics* "a branch of mechanics that deals with forces and their relation primarily to motion but sometimes also to the equilibrium of bodies." The second meaning given reads more simply: "the pattern of change or growth of an object or phenomenon." Although the idea of "pattern of change or growth" seems readily applicable to the Exercises, we can also work with an adaptation of the notion of "forces related to motion and to balance." We need to keep both of these meanings in mind when we speak of "the *dynamics* of the Spiritual Exercises."

By choosing the word *exercises* as part of his book title, Ignatius has laid the groundwork for our tracing such *dynamics* as we discover them in the context of his book. Ignatius emphasizes that the kind of book he is writing is one focused, not on content matter, but rather on movement, development, or growth, especially as these words apply to insights and

---

in the life of Jesus as reported in the different Gospels" ("The Call to Discipleship: The Spiritual Exercises with the Gospel of St. Mark," *The Way Supplement,* no. 43-44 [Jan. 1982]: 13).

affections. The word *dynamics* also refers to the Ignatian order or arrangement—perhaps more accurately described, using the active verbal form, as ordering or arranging—that provides the kind of balance evident throughout the Exercises. The concept of dynamics is integral to the Ignatian notion of the providence of God—"God arranging all things sweetly."[3] The word *dynamics* also deals with the idea of a power or power source. This notion of dynamics we will also see in the course of the Exercises, especially in the interplay between memory and imagination, both integral to Ignatian prayer and discernment.

The word *dynamics* applies most basically to the overall makeup of the Exercises. We will find such dynamics writ large as we look first at the movement within a retreat day, then at the movement within a Week, and finally at the Ignatian movement threading through all the Weeks that comprise the full Exercises.

The Dynamics within Each Day

If we remember that the retreatant's exercising is essential to the Ignatian retreat, then we recognize that the movement within each day is from more activity to less activity. In the usual pattern of the thirty-day retreat, each day begins with two prayer periods, each one having different content matter. Then follows a third prayer exercise, which Ignatius calls a *repetition*. A possible fourth period is again a kind of repetition, and finally comes a fifth and last prayer period, usually identified by Ignatius as an *application of the senses*.

Ignatius suggests that each prayer period be followed by a short period of examination, reviewing how the period progressed. By means of this examination, Ignatius filters the original content material of the day's first two prayer exercises, not so much through noting ideas as through paying attention to insights and affective movements.[4] As we move into the later prayer periods of the day, identified by Ignatius as a *repetition* and then as a *résumé*, we observe that he is not telling us to repeat the content matter.

---

[3] Gilles Cusson describes this providence as our being caught up in God's plan of salvation (Gilles Cusson, SJ, *Biblical Theology and the Spiritual Exercises* [St. Louis: Institute of Jesuit Sources, 1988]).

[4] "Marking and dwelling on the points in which I have felt greater consolation or desolation, or greater spiritual feeling" [63].

Rather he asks that we return in our repetition-prayer exercise to those moments in our previous prayer periods when we were moved by an insight or when we found a positive affective response of attraction or a negative one of avoidance. Ignatius, in one of his early notes [6] at the beginning of the *Spiritual Exercises* book, directs the one giving the retreat to ask questions of the retreatant if there should seem to be a lack of movement in the prayer periods of the day.

The final prayer period of the day, usually identified as the *application of the senses*, is not meant to be the introduction of a new way of praying. If we were to actively engage ourselves in a new way of praying in the final prayer period of a retreat day, we would have to be stirring ourselves up to a fresh activity when in fact the day has been structured towards a gradual quieting down and a deepening movement. In using the descriptive words *application of senses*, Ignatius stresses and highlights the passive way that our senses take in the world around us. When we enter into the final prayer period of the day, we are allowing what has been our prayer world of this day to be present to us in a way similar to the way that the sensible world impresses itself upon us. We are truly "actively passive"—or "attentively passive"—in this prayer period.

The more we take literally the directions for seeing, hearing, smelling, tasting, and touching, and accordingly take on, one by one, each sense experience, the further we may be distancing ourselves from the passive approach that Ignatius seems to intend in this way of praying. For there also exists in our Christian prayer tradition an active way to pray using the senses, and naturally this way of praying requires a more concentrated effort, a real "working at it." For example, this way of actively "working at" a method of praying through the senses is reflected in the Ignatian *language* of the fifth prayer period of the First Week, called a "meditation on hell" [65]. Yet, in a seeming paradox, Ignatius does not use the words *application of the senses* in this instance, but only in the fifth and final prayer periods of the Second, Third, and Fourth Weeks. I believe that the nonuse of the descriptive "application of the senses" for this First Week prayer is significant.

Ignatius is careful to explain, however briefly, different ways of praying in the First and Second Weeks. In seeking to help the retreatant to enter into an experience of hell, Ignatius seemingly encourages us, by means of his choice of language, to work with our imagination at seeing great fires, at hearing wailings and cries, at smelling putrid things, at tasting tears and sadness, and at touching the burning sensation. This exercise relates us to the way our senses take in data, but it also appears to emphasize that we actively stir up this kind of sense activity. However, from the evidence we have of the way that the prayer moves within a day and from our experience of receptor senses, it seems that Ignatius is pointing to a more nuanced understanding of the prayer called the *application of the senses*. We can see, for example, that "tasting sadness" is not a physical sense experience, and so Ignatius is indicating that we do not take literally the idea of "application of the senses." As usual, Ignatius presumes that the experience of the director will let Ignatius's words "point" (that is, "give direction") and not prescribe how this prayer period proceeds.

The director, from the knowledge he or she has gained experientially from making the Exercises, is familiar with the Ignatian description given in the Second Week for the application-of-the-senses prayer period that emphasizes the movement of "reflecting within oneself" (*reflectiendo en si mismo*) [123, 124]. Ignatius is reminding the director that, in-the-application-of-the-senses prayer, the direction of such reflecting is inward (following the same dynamics as the repetitions), not toward experiencing new input from outside the retreatant.

What is being emphasized by Ignatius is our full body-and-soul involvement—our being actively passive—in the final prayer period of the day. It is like having all the prayer highlights of the day cascade over us in a drenching shower; it is akin to what we call an "overload of sensible experiences." The fifth prayer period of the First Week, then, can be understood as an *experience* of hell—in the manner that each sense makes real the concrete experience—if we let ourselves be immersed in the sin experience we have had through the four previous prayer periods of the day. *That* experience of the retreatant will likely bring hell far closer as a reality than any imaginative objectifying of a place of torment.

The Ignatian prayer day, then, moves from an active involvement with the prayer's content material through a progressive distillation of its graced meaning and affect to a kind of resolution of ourselves immersed within the day's prayer more by God's grace than by our effort. As we know from the single day described as making up the First Week, sometimes the quieting progression of a single day still leaves much personal interior work to be done in succeeding days. But the ideal of a retreat day's movement remains constant—from more activity to less, even to quiet resting. We need only note that we will see the one exception made by Ignatius to this daily pattern, namely, the Fourth Day of the Second Week.

The Dynamics within Each Week

The movement within each Week follows the same pattern: greater activity at the beginning of the Week and a progressively quieter affect as the Week comes to a close. We retreatants find that our prayer seems to grow simpler and quieter as the Week progresses. The experience of a growing calm in the one making the retreat is a sign to the director that the Week is coming to a close and that the grace prayed for has been received.

Although the Second Week remains true to this kind of movement, it does have a greater number of distinctive parts disrupting the movement's flow than any other Week. During the first three days or so of the Second Week, we are being introduced to a new way of praying—contemplation. Whether it is two or three or more days, Ignatius wants to give time for retreatants to learn how to be as still and reflectively observant as this kind of praying demands. Ignatian contemplation is quite different from the meditation style of the first two content prayer periods described in the First Week. Contemplation also differs from the consideration, or rumination, style of the Principle and Foundation and the Call of the King. In chapter 5, we will further distinguish Ignatian contemplation from other ways of praying. The first part of the Second Week lasts just long enough for the director to be able to sense that the retreatant has worked at and developed an easy familiarity with this type of Gospel praying.

Ignatius then inserts the Fourth Day. The Fourth Day presents us with different dynamics. It is a day of total activity—all meditations. Ignatius suggests that we meditate on the Two Standards twice; in other words, he is asking the retreatant to use the same material two times (thus distinguishing the second exercise from a repetition), working through the material in a meditative way.[5] Then he proposes two repetitions. Since we are praying for the grace of understanding, we expect the emphasis within the repetitions to be more on insight than on affect. What is most surprising is that wholly new matter is presented for the fifth and final prayer exercise. Once again a

---

[5] "This exercise will be made at midnight and then a second time in the morning, and two repetitions of this same will be made" [148].

meditation is put forward, a meditation entitled Three Types of Persons (traditionally called The Three Classes of Men). The Fourth Day is unique in its demand for the retreatant to be active, in the meditative style, through all five prayer periods of the day.

Although the movement of the Second Week returns to Gospel contemplation as its way of praying from the Fifth Day onward, there is the added busyness of the consideration of the Three Degrees of Humility outside of the ordinary prayer times and the possible election consideration. The rumination on the Three Degrees of Humility may last some days, and then, through prayer, it blends into the sensitizing readiness that prepares the retreatant to come to a decision. The Second Week is known to come to its conclusion when there is quiet in the retreatant, a quiet that comes with a decision being made or with the resolution of closeness to Jesus drawing the retreatant into the Third Degree of Humility. The Second Week, like the First Week, ends with a movement towards quiet and peace.

The movement in the Third and Fourth Weeks remains consistently straightforward. Throughout the Third Week, the Gospel-contemplative way of praying is retained. Following the ordinary format, each day begins with two prayer periods containing Gospel passages, continues with periods of repetitions, and concludes with a period of the application of the senses. However, a difference is introduced: Ignatius now gives the director greater freedom to suggest optional alternatives in the retreatant's prayer, especially in the last three days of the Week. Ignatius proposes as one option that the passion narrative could be read in two parts over two days and then read as a whole on the third day, letting the passage permeate the whole day's prayer. Then, looking at the Week as a whole, he allows another alternative format—a different Gospel passage may be the content for each prayer period, without any repetition or application of the senses. In this format he again suggests closing the Week with the prayer day permeated by a reading of the whole passion. The Third Week ends with the somber quiet of being with Jesus in the tomb and staying with the empty loneliness of Mary and the apostles.

The Fourth Week follows the general movement from much activity to a quiet rest. There is, however, a major change in the Fourth Week: Ignatius directs that each prayer exercise should have its own content matter. As we have noted above, Ignatius has allowed for this possibility in the Third Week. In the Fourth Week, it becomes his only direction for the movement of the Week. The difference seems to be that he allows for an application of the senses in the final prayer period of the day. In the Ignatian text, with the Gospel contemplations flowing through the three or four prayer periods of each day, there is no hint given about how the Contemplation on the Love of God is to be integrated into the Week.

After Ignatius was so careful in the first two Weeks of the Exercises not to overwhelm the retreatant with content matter, restricting the content to the first two prayer periods, we may ask ourselves why Ignatius would suggest a different Scripture passage for each period in the Fourth Week (and allow for the possibility in the Third Week too). In the Fourth Week, we focus on Jesus as Consoler, no matter what the post-resurrection situation. Ignatius would have us see that the passage itself does not weigh us down with new thought or feeling. Always our single focus is on Jesus in his consoling role. In a similar way, we can say that the passages on his passion have us focus not on the different situations but rather on the interior disposition of Jesus. We are given indication of this in the Third Week in the Ignatian addition of three more points for each prayer period. The three added points for each prayer exercise in the Third Week look towards our letting Jesus help us enter into his feelings, much as the added two points for the prayer periods in the Fourth Week point to a similar inward movement.

From the early directories, written as helps in giving the Exercises, we have evidence that the Contemplation on the Love of God can be integrated into the retreat in a number of ways. Just as the passion narrative, as a whole or in parts, could be the content of our prayer exercises during the last three days of the Third Week, so too the Contemplation on the Love of God has been described traditionally as the content of the last days of the retreat. Another practice would be to use the Contemplation, as a whole or in its parts, as the final prayer period of each day in the Fourth Week, with the possibility of the final day taking in the whole of the Contemplation. The consoling action of the risen Christ is brought home to us in the "now" activity of our loving God given in each of the Contemplation's four points. We are meant to see a continuity between the activity of Jesus the Consoler seen in each day's Scripture passages, and the daily activity of God communicating his love. The Contemplation is seen, then, not as a pull-out-all-the-stops organ crescendo closing the retreat, but as the natural flow of the activity of Jesus the Consoler into the so-called Fifth Week (the "beyond") of our ordinary human life. Once again we see how the Fourth

Week comes to a peace-and-quiet consolation in the retreatant, even though this Week clearly does not have the same feel of a conclusion as did the other Weeks. The Fourth Week moves us out into ordinary life, where we ourselves no longer feel so ordinary.

The dynamics or movement within each Week seems evident. Every Week tends to begin with greater activity on the part of the retreatant; then as the Week progresses, the retreatant comes to be quieter and more at peace, these very dynamics signifying that the Week itself is coming to a close. For Ignatius, then, a *Week* is not based on any number of days, as he has called to our attention in his introductory observations [4]. An Ignatian *Week* takes its shape from the dynamics of a more active to less active movement in the retreatant, a movement facilitated by the careful directions given by Ignatius and adapted by the director for a particular retreatant.

The Dynamics between the Weeks

We are accustomed to saying that each Week of the Exercises has its own grace. The grace of a particular Week has been described in various ways by different commentators on the Exercises. The asking-for-the-grace prelude—usually the second (as in the First Week) or the third prelude (as commonly seen in the other Weeks)—is an essential in the Ignatian structure of a prayer period. The grace prelude, when taken in conjunction with what Ignatius calls a *colloquy*, gives us another indication of movement in the Ignatian retreat and is an essential in its dynamics. A retreat director asks the retreatant to look back over the past day and reflect: What grace did I pray for? What grace did I receive? The director's role is to hear, to clarify, and to identify God's gifting to the retreatant; these actions are a necessary step in setting the direction of the next retreat day—giving thanks for the grace received and petitioning for the grace now to be sought. It is from monitoring how the grace received each day progresses to the grace of each subsequent day that a director begins to sense how the grace of the Week is taking shape in a retreatant. The dynamic interplay between the grace prelude (what we desire) and the colloquy (what relationship with God we are enjoying) ultimately indicates when a retreatant has reached some conclusion to a Week's work. We will see in chapter 6 a further development—greater focuson the relationship (in the colloquy) than on naming the grace prayed for.

The Week-to-Week flow of grace received might be described in a way analogous to a psychological model of adult development; as with the stages of adult development, the stages of one's spiritual development are not skipped. For example, if a person were forced, or forced himself or herself, to a more mature stage of development than personal age, circumstance, and maturity naturally called for or allowed, then usually there comes a retrogression at some point in that person's life (perhaps years later) that requires some make-up work. During the Exercises, we see spiritual growth in terms of grace received, and that involves a natural progression that cannot be forced, so that we can truly say that grace builds upon grace.

In the First Week, there is the grace of clarifying our relationship with God beyond the foundational God who creates and gifts us out of love. In the First Week, we come to know this God, through the face of Jesus on the Cross, as our redeemer, a redeemer whose justice and mercy are caught up in a forgiving love, no matter what our sinful response to God and to God's gifts. Proceeding from the Principle and Foundation through the First Week, we experience the grace of being gifted, forgiven, and loved. We are the recipients of God's saving work. We rest in the felt knowledge that we are at once gifted, loved, sinful, and saved.

In the Second Week, we hear the call and invitation to be companions with Christ in the work of salvation. We are invited to labor, to serve, even to suffer, but always *with* Christ. Since all the events of our life are to be in union *with* Christ, we enter into the prayer exercises of the Second Week, with our focus on seeking the grace to better know and love Jesus in order to follow him more closely. As the Week progresses, we seek the grace to follow God's lead in making our life decisions, just as Jesus did in his life. We acknowledge that the grace sought is first of all to be in a relationship— knowing and loving Jesus—and secondly, as an integral part of this deepening relationship, to be enabled to labor and serve. As a result, the choices and decisions about service and work are viewed through the lenses of Christ's values (the Two Standards) and of Christ's way of making decisions in his life (Ignatian contemplations), along with our consideration of the Degrees of Humility, which promote our resolve about how closely we identify with Jesus. The Second Week centers us on the movement in which Jesus draws us closer in friendship to be busy with him about the reign of God.

In the Third Week, Christ remains the focus, but there is a change from the *doing with* Christ to a *being with* him. *Compassion* is a summary word designating the grace of this Week, a week devoted to the events from Holy Thursday through Holy Saturday. We seek the grace to *be with* or to *stay with* Christ in his greatest work, the work for which he was born. Yet, as is typical of a Gospel paradox, this *work* focuses, not on his activity, but rather on what happens to him. In John's gospel, Jesus raises the question: "Should I ask that the Father save me from this hour?" And then he goes on immediately to answer his own question; "But it is for this hour that I was sent" (Jn 12:27).

In a similar way, we experience a question rising within us about staying with Jesus at this time of his passion. His passion is history; we can do nothing to change it. We want to escape from a painful situation where we seemingly can do nothing. Ignatius strongly emphasizes how we must "labor" in our praying in this Week. Compassion is hard because it results only in our involved presence, when relieving action on our part is impossible or negligible. As we allow Jesus to help us enter into his passion, we find that the grace of compassion leads to a new depth of relationship with Jesus. We experience that the love of compassion must be an integral part of the love of service. We have moved beyond the *service or working with Jesus* of the Second Week. Through this Third Week, *labor* in a faith perspective has shattered our simple notions of work, of what is valued, and of accomplishments. Only on the cross, Jesus can say, "It is finished, the work that I have been sent to do."

Sometimes it is stated that the grace of the Third Week is the confirmation of the Second Week. Although there is some element of truth being pointed to, such a restrictive understanding of the grace of this Week misses a most precious development in our growth in Christ. The Third Week grace helps us enter into a new depth of relationship with Christ that reorders our values about our own work and activity with Christ. The Second Week grace by itself cannot balance the movement of an apostolic life in its following of Christ. The Third Week grace is essential to the dynamics of an apostolic life. It can be known only in the graced experience of compassion.

In the Fourth Week, we find ourselves praying for the grace to enter into Christ's joy in his resurrection victory and to know him in his role as Consoler. We are touching into the flip side of the grace of compassion. Just as previously we were the ones who were being gifted with the grace of an active compassion, a following and commiserating with Christ in his passion and death, so now we want the grace of a more passive experience, the grace of being consoled by Christ, a consolation that Christ is always giving us through his loving presence, whatever the circumstances of our life. Just as we do not change Jesus' history by our compassionate presence, so ordinarily Jesus does not change our life history by his resurrection presence. But the risen Christ impresses on us that he is always present with his consolation, strengthening us and even giving us joy in situations both pleasant and straitened. Saints have evidenced for us this kind of consolation given them by Jesus in hard times and even in suffering leading to death. In the Third Week, we entered into the graced experience of being compassionately present with Christ in his passion. In the Fourth Week, we come to see from our graced experience how Jesus always stands close to us as a consoling presence, no matter what the circumstances of our life. In the dynamics present between the Third and Fourth Weeks we see clearly the movement of grace building upon grace.

Although the Contemplation on the Love of God is an integral part of the Fourth Week, the focus of its dynamics is definitely beyond the retreat. I prefer the interpretation of this prayer exercise as a recapitulation of finding God in all things, reviewed through the experiences of the Four Weeks. We are graced with an awe, a reverence for God's omnipresence, a presence which we have experienced in the various movements of the Weeks: in our being created, in our being gifted, in our being forgiven as sinners, in our being called by Christ and in our following him, in our serving, in our being compassionate with Christ, and in our being consoled by Christ. We recognize God, active and working with us and our world, communicating his love. Empowered by this retreat experience of God's engulfing love, we are confident of similar graces to live our everyday life.

Evidencing Other Dynamics

If we keep in mind that Ignatius is presenting us with an exercise book, we will not be surprised that every aspect of its makeup is affected by movement. I want to point out some of the other *forces* or *dynamics* that contribute to the overall dynamics of the Exercises. Ignatius uses a teaching method of moving from an objective reading to a subjective application. A ready example is provided in the first and second exercises of the First

Week. In the first exercise we are meditating on objective instances of sin in order to come to a sense of the evil of a single bad act. When the awfulness of sin itself hits home, then we can look at our own life and where sin has infected it. The movement from objective to subjective recalls the famous Biblical example of the prophet Nathan telling David about a rich man, not taking from his own flocks, but selecting a poor servant's only lamb to serve his guests a meal. David, in his anger at the wrong being committed, is confounded when Nathan simply states, "You are the one" (2 Sm 12:1-7). David knows the story's application without further explanation.

The movement from objective to subjective can be found in subtle ways throughout the Exercises. The opening paragraphs of the Principle and Foundation begin objectively with the creation of "man"—not the philosophical human composite, but the concrete "everyman." In the final paragraph Ignatius switches to a subjective perspective with "we." In the Call of the King, Ignatius suggests no colloquy, but instead has us be present to a kind of *colloquy prayer* of the generous, great-souled persons who want to respond. At this point of the retreat, a seed of what is the generous response is being planted, even though we may not be ready to involve ourselves subjectively. The Three Types of Persons (Three Classes of Men) is similar to a case study inasmuch as its methodology allows us to look at a situation objectively and so not feel personally involved or threatened. In the Second Way to Make a Good and Sound Election [184], Ignatius again employs the objective-subjective dynamics; he suggests that we imagine ourselves trying to give advice to another and then following the advice we would give to that person. Ignatian contemplation allows us to take a certain objective stance when we see, hear, and observe, though always with the intention to be personally involved and thus also able to become a subjective participant in the scene. The particular dynamics between the objective and the subjective plays an important part in an Ignatian retreat's progress.

There is also the dynamics of the personal focus moving to the communal. In the Principle and Foundation, we have found our grounding in a personal relationship (the objective everyman is an individual person, an "I"), but in one subtly expressed in the last paragraph as a "we" situation of choice. The personal moving to the communal is more explicitly imaged in the Call of the King, where the call comes to every man, woman, and child, and the call comes to each of us personally. But Jesus obviously invites us in our personal relationship with him to work with others similarly called. In both the Two Standards and the Three Types of Persons, we are aware of our own personal involvement, and at the same time we know that our involvement with others takes on Jesus' values and acts on them. Finally the movement from personal to communal is presented in its fullness in the Contemplation on the Love of God. When the Ignatian *prenote* highlights communication as being central to love, we are presented with a way of living that involves all the ways of sharing what one has and has by gift, just as God shares with all in his gifting.

Since Ignatius has written an exercise book, ways of viewing its various movements or dynamics permeate the text. We have considered some of the major movements essential to the very structuring of the Exercises. We have also looked at other more subtle dynamics that enhance the progress of the Ignatian retreat. As Ignatius points out in the Second Annotation, the emphasis is not on content. The Exercises have, above all, the overall dynamics that facilitate our welcoming God into the depth of our being. Only when we do that is the paradox of the divine dynamics realized: God is the first to welcome, and through his sharing helps us enter into the Trinitarian life.

Chapter Three

REMEMBERING AND IMAGINING

Outstanding in the dynamics of the Spiritual Exercises are the two elements of memory and imagination.[1] Because Ignatius has written an *exercise* book, these two aspects are better expressed actively by the words *remembering* and *imagining*. Remembering and imagining are like the twin pistons that drive a steamboat forward. If only one is working, the boat goes in circles. If one piston pulls too hard, the boat is driven off the main channel and may go aground. But if both pistons are pulling equally well, the boat moves forward with smooth speed. Remembering and imagining act like pistons in the movement of the Exercises.

Remembering

We associate the word *remembering* with Ignatius's use of *memory* to describe one of the aspects of our way of praying. In the meditation form of prayer found in the Exercises, especially in the First Week, Ignatius refers to the use of memory, understanding, and will—traditional ways of describing our human faculties used in the process of this form of praying. In Ignatius's directions for praying the Gospel contemplations found in the Second, Third, and Fourth Weeks of the Exercises, we again note his insistence on recalling or remembering the Gospel passages that he gives for this particular prayer time. Since people did not often have Bibles for their personal use in the first one hundred years or more of Jesuit retreat giving, memory played an important role when the Ignatian director was recalling the Gospel mystery. The Gospel stories took their place alongside of the director's other stories, to be told and to be remembered—all for the progress of the retreat.

---

[1] The ideas developed in this chapter were first presented at the Ignatian Spirituality Conference at Saint Louis University in July 2002. The talk was later published in *Review for Religious* 62, no. 6 (Nov.-Dec. 2002). Again the ideas here presented took shape as a chapter titled "Keys to Spiritual Growth: Remembering and Imagining in Ignatian Spirituality" in Thomas M. Lucas, SJ, ed., *Spirit, Style, Story: Essays Honoring John W. Padberg, SJ* (Chicago: Loyola Press, 2002).

Remembering so permeates Ignatian spirituality that it can be well characterized as a *reflective* spirituality. Some people are not naturally reflective and, even with training, are little inclined to a process of reflection; such people do not find a home in Ignatian spirituality. Ever since the now classic article "The Examen of Consciousness" by Father George Aschenbrenner was published in the journal *Review for Religious* in 1972, this element of Ignatian spirituality has been the subject of a number of books and articles.

The Examen

In fact, one indication of the central importance of remembering is found in the Ignatian stress on examination as a spiritual exercise. Ignatius more often describes this exercise of reviewing one's activities both in praying and in daily living by his favored shortened expression, transliterated into English as *examen*. We mark that Ignatius begins the text of the First Week not with content matter for meditation, but rather with an explanation of various kinds of examens. In this way he gives a hint right at the beginning for the one making the Exercises that his approach to spirituality demands that one be reflective. A person should be able to look back, to recall thoughts and interior movements, to remember insights and stirring desires.

Ignatius suggests that making the examen every day is important; in fact, he proposes that about midday and again at the end of the day one should spend some time (identified as a quarter of an hour) in this kind of review of where God has been present or absent in one's day. One can also make a *particular* examen within the daily examen: an examination on a focused area of one's life, for example, a virtue to be practiced so as to make it one's own, by God's grace, or a fault to be overcome, again by God's grace inspiring and strengthening one's effort. Neither of these examens is restricted to a retreat time, but rather both are meant to be a daily part of one's life with God. In addition, Ignatius recalls the traditional examination of conscience to prepare oneself for the sacrament of reconciliation, whether exercised in its regular rhythm of church life or in its special use when one makes a general confession of one's life, especially in the context of the thirty-day retreat experience.

As we move into the prayer periods of the retreat described in Ignatius's *Spiritual Exercises*, we find himagain stressing the importance of a time for an examen upon completion of a prayer period. Rather than letting us get distracted by a focusing on our own responses during our prayer, Ignatius suggests that we devote some time shortly after finishing our formal prayer period—marked by a different bodily position, like sitting or walking if we have been praying in a kneeling or standing state—to reflecting on where God has met us in *this* prayer time, on what our own response or lack of response has been, and on what other movements we discover as we look back over our prayer time. For Ignatius, this kind of examen of our formal prayer period serves both to provide the matter for the daily conference with the retreat director and to ensure that a prayer period can build upon the graced experience of the previous one.

As a general overview about the use of memory, these are some of the favored ways that remembering is effected in the Ignatian Exercises. There is no doubt that Ignatian spirituality finds its home in a reflective person.

Imagining

If the action of looking back or reviewing is easily associated with Ignatian spirituality, Ignatius's stress on the use of imagination may not come so readily to mind. From a cursory reading, the text of the *Spiritual Exercises* book may seem dry, almost telegram like in expression, with little colorful or emotive language. But Ignatius indicates, although subtly, at the very beginning of the text that he assumes a director who uses imagination. That the *Spiritual Exercises* book begins with a section called *Annotations* is significant. By beginning the text with this section containing directions for the retreat director, Ignatius makes clear that the Exercises in practice must always be adapted to the one(s) making the retreat. He is emphasizing that the director's own imaginative adaptation and application is necessary for the good movement of the retreat. Yet the most evident call upon imagination is found in the consistent way in which Ignatius approaches the mysteries of Jesus' life as presented in the Gospels.

Ignatian Contemplation

Although Ignatius is not usually identified with original spiritual practices, his way of entering into prayer on the Gospel mysteries of Jesus' life has led to his being credited with a prayer method known as Ignatian contemplation. We find an explanation of this way of praying as we enter into the Second Week of the Exercises.

Ignatius presents us with two approaches to this way of praying that draw upon our imagination. In the first contemplation of the first day of the Second Week, Ignatius indicates that we see, meshing our gaze with the gaze of our triune God, first, the world in its mix of peoples and their relationships and, second, Mary and the angel Gabriel and their conversation about God's intention of becoming a human being. Along with God, we are deeply moved by the plight of those peopling our earthly globe, and again with God we wait expectantly for Mary's response so that we may acknowledge with great wonder the decisive moment of God's Word made flesh.

In the second contemplation Ignatius suggests the same kind of intimate involvement in the mystery under consideration, but our involvement is *from within* rather than that previously described as *from above*.[2] When we consider the Gospel nativity scene, we are encouraged to take our place as a participant in the events described. Ignatius suggests that we might imagine ourselves in the role of a servant ready to be helpful to Joseph and Mary in doing whatever they might ask of us. With these two relatively brief indications of how to enter into this kind of Gospel contemplation, Ignatius presumes that he has given the retreatant enough help, along with the director's continuing guidance, to enter into this form of contemplation in the Second Week.

In broad strokes, then, we have portrayed two central elements of the Exercises' dynamics: the element of remembering, especially as used in the reflective examen, which consistently permeates the Exercises, and the element of imagining, especially as employed in the way of praying the Ignatian contemplations found in the Second, Third, and Fourth Weeks of the retreat. To appreciate the dynamism these two elements have provided to this spiritual approach, it is important for us to trace more carefully the interplay between remembering and imagining throughout the text of the *Spiritual Exercises* book and the experience it engenders.

---

[2] Hugo Rahner, SJ, used this kind of distinction for the two approaches to contemplation described by Ignatius. See his *Ignatius the Theologian* (London: Geoffrey Chapman, 1968).

Four-Week Movement

The progress of the retreat in the full thirty-day experience of the Spiritual Exercises is found in the movement relating one Week to another—what we have traditionally identified as "grace building upon grace." We need to remember how God has worked with us in the Week just completed in order to be more readily available for his continuing guidance in our life. In terms of our Judeo-Christian heritage, each of us enters into the Israelite experience of needing to look back at—to remember—God's ways of acting so that those past ways might shed light on our present and future directions. The Bible is a memory document, and through its God-given light, memory or *re-membering* serves an important role in allowing us to gather and "put together" our experiences in their relation to God. As Ignatius has framed each day and each Week of his Exercises, remembering is meant to give us a God perspective, not locking us into a personal response that is merely a reaction to the anonymous "what happens."

A. The First Week

The movement from the Principle and Foundation consideration to the First Week exercises takes place as a natural flow because of human memory. As we reflect on our Judeo-Christian vision of God and of ourselves and of our world and consider our responsibility to make choices in the context of goods which are meant to help lead us to God, we find ourselves remembering not only our delight in these gifts but also our misuse of God's gifts. This natural movement of memory leads us, with a director's guidance, into the first exercise, a meditation which is on sin as the rejection of God—a rejection made clearly visible by our recalling the choices of the first free creatures of God's creation, angels and human beings. From the recall and pondering of these *objective* biblical stories, we progress to the second meditation, which is the *subjective* consideration of our own life. Ignatius gives us the memory helps of (1) places we have lived; (2) the people we have dealt with; and (3) the occupations or responsibilities we have held, so that we can more easily recollect in what ways we have sinned and rejected God.

In the first prelude of each prayer time in the First Week, Ignatius calls us to a *composition*. This composition we enter into through the *seeing* of the imagination—seeing a physical setting if that is the reality or seeing a metaphorical setting if it is an abstract context. The emphasis here is not just on a physical setting like our setting up stage scenery. Ignatius rather stresses the imaginative way of composing our very being, that is, positioning *ourselves*, in a felt way consistent with our prayer content. The composition prelude serves as a centering element of our whole being with the content matter of Ignatian prayer.

In the indicated colloquy of the first exercise, Ignatius, with a few carefully chosen words, paints a picture of Christ on the cross, the Christ who is the Word through whom "all things came into being, and apart from [whom] nothing came to be" (Jn 1:3). This description of Christ described as *Creator*, even while he hangs on a cross, is in keeping with the focus of the Principle and Foundation and the creation stories of angels and first parents. To the mystery of evil, this Creator God responds, in continuing love, with the mystery of the cross.

In the Ignatian meditations of the First Week, we do not pray for the grace to understand evil and sin; evil and sin remain mystery. Instead we pray for the grace of shame and confusion—because we do not understand others, such as Adam and Eve and the angels, and their behavior in the face of God's loving goodness, or even ourselves and our own inability to act with consistency in doing the good. In the second prayer period, as we look to our own life, we pray for the grace of sorrow, even to the point of tears, over our sinful response to God. The shame and confusion, the sorrow and tears, with which God's grace gifts us, are embedded in the foundational response of our gratitude to God. Gratitude is the permeating response of the First Week prayer—a gratitude to a God who never stops loving us and providing the gifts of love.

The imaginative placing of ourselves before Christ on his cross provides the setting which opens up that personal conversation between God and ourselves, about evil and sin, our own part in it, and God's response. We realize that the grace prelude and the colloquy are two interlocked elements where Ignatius finds an engine for the movement within the retreat day and Week. Through the grace prelude (what we desire) and the colloquy (what relationship with God we enjoy) we subtly become participants in an Ignatian pattern that opens us to a future in which we make ourselves available to God.

The matter or content of the next two prayer exercises in the Ignatian text flows from the examens we have done after completing the previous prayer exercises. In each examen following upon the prayer period, we are directed to note where we have felt moved either by greater consolation or desolation or, in general, greater spiritual appreciation. These movements and the thoughts that have elicited them, which we have remembered and then noted down, provide the content matter of the third prayer exercise. Ignatius identifies this prayer period as a *repetition*, and he makes frequent use of this manner of praying throughout the Weeks of the Exercises.

The fourth prayer exercise of this First Week is identified as a repetition of the previous period. Ignatius makes the content of this fourth prayer period once again what we have remembered as significant movements of the previous repetition. The Ignatian repetition always starts from the thoughts or feelings that have been significant in the preceding prayer experience—and then from *this* starting point we come to see where God will continue to lead and interact with us. As a result, there is both a remembering aspect (a going back to a previous response) and an imaginative one (an openness to the new, a future not within our control) in the Ignatian repetition.

In the fifth and final prayer exercise of the First Week, Ignatius has us enter into an imaginative experience of hell. We have touched on this in the previous chapter, but it is important to review it once again in the context of remembering and imagining. There have always been differing interpretations about the makeup of this imagining, since Ignatius in the other Weeks will refer to this final prayer period as an Application of the Senses. Some would say that Ignatius is much more centered on imagining with the true physical senses, granted some metaphorical use of tasting the bitterness of tears and sorrow. Others would point out rather that Ignatius is alluding to the spiritual senses, after the manner of the descriptions given in the spiritual writings of the Franciscan St. Bonaventure.

If we note the simplifying—or what we might describe as the "distilling process" of prayer—that is evident in the Ignatian use of repetition, it would be jarring to introduce a new kind of prayer which would demand a lot of activity at the end of the day. More in keeping with Ignatius's movement is an explanation that sees this fifth and last prayer period of the day (which, for the first time in this First Week's meditation prayer pattern, calls for a prayer of imagination) as a more passive way of praying. By alluding to our common experience of sense awareness, Ignatius indicates how we allow the total experience of all our prayer times of *this* day to sweep over us just as our senses drink in the total environment without the necessity of any intentional effort on our part. The prayer matter—thoughts and feelings—is not new and requires no new effort on our part. We let ourselves be immersed in what has involved us during this retreat day, and it becomes our own imaginative experience of hell.

No matter how we understand this imagination prayer to be identified with sense experience, I want us to turn our attention to the directions which Ignatius gives for the colloquy—the interchange with God or what we might label as the "actual praying" time. He suggests that we bring to mind people of the ages before Jesus' coming who chose hell by what they did or failed to do, people of Jesus' lifetime who similarly chose hell, and finally people who have continued to choose hell by their sins of commission or their sins of omission in every age since Jesus' resurrection. Recalling such people, we can only give thanks for God's mercy, experienced in Christ, up to this moment in our life. With this kind of remembering and imagining exercise, the material content of the First Week closes.

Although there can be times of imagination, as in the prayer period on hell, the First Week stresses exercises more evidently using the memory. Remembering is urged because there is no moving forward unless we are aware of and accept the past that is ours. Remembering, for Ignatius, is never a nostalgic time. It is rather a time to look for God's footprints, a time to glimpse the devil's tail, a time to note our own past blindness or insensitivity to God's gifts or God's action in our life. Noting that God's response to sin and evil is Jesus on the cross and is thereby in continuity with Love's outpouring of gifts upon us, we experience the grace of being the loved and forgiven sinner. We have come to know the justice of God in his loving mercy. Only by taking the time to remember God's response can we choose to act differently—with gratitude. Remembering always remains essential in shaping the Ignatian imaginative choosing of a future.

B. The Second Week

Just as we consider the Principle and Foundation as part of the First Week movement, so we may see the Call of the King as introductory to, but a part of, the Second Week movement. There is a long tradition among Ignatian commentators to identify the Call of the King as a second Principle and Foundation. It is true that it fits more the consideration model of the Principle and Foundation inasmuch as Ignatius himself suggests no colloquy or proper praying time in either exercise. Just as the Principle and Foundation leads naturally into the exercises of the First Week, so too the Call of the King flows in a similar way into the consideration of the mysteries of Christ's life. If we pray for the grace not to be deaf to Christ's call in our own life, we find the stirrings of the desire to know him better so that we may be able to follow him more surely.

The comparison that Ignatius draws between the temporal king and Christ our Lord is based upon a summary picture of Jesus taken from the Gospels. Ignatius wants us to remember the calls of Jesus and his desire to have followers whose lives, like his, are concerned with God and the coming of God's kingdom. Although Ignatius could have chosen a particular Gospel passage that seemed to sum up Jesus' call and identity of mission (for example, Mt 28:16-20), he instead imaginatively paints his own synopsis picture of Jesus' making his call to every man, woman, and child. He has the risen Jesus (the *now* Jesus) issue a biblical battle cry—the battle being against evil in all its forms of death-dealing to God's creation, especially to humankind. Ignatius is touching into the imaginative stirrings of the human heart toward a vision and a mission that is worth the spending of one's life.

This structural piece is an exercise that is imaginative in a number of ways. First, in a flow from our First Week experience, this exercise well fulfills the idea of a mercy meditation. Our saving God does not let us be the passive recipients of his merciful justice. Christian salvation is not limited to a "saving from" sin. Rather the salvation offered by God in Christ is the very empowering of God's own life in us so that we may live as the sons and daughters God has created us to be. In this Ignatian exercise, through our Savior's invitation we are welcomed to be participants in the salvation mission. We observe imaginatively people responding in two different ways— some logically or rationally and others generously or magnanimously. Ignatius is very careful not to ask us as retreatants to make our own response at this time. We need to know more about Jesus and what his call to us entails. And so our desires are naturally led to the contemplations of Jesus' life. The Call of the King is functioning both as a conclusion to the First Week of experiencing God's merciful justice and as a foundation of the Second Week and beyond for all the contemplations of Jesus' life. Here, between the First and Second Weeks, this exercise dramatically serves as a concrete instance of a grace building upon a grace.

Second, this exercise is imaginative in its Ignatian presentation. When we do not appreciate the Ignatian emphasis on imagination, we easily lose the "magic" that his structural piece had for his contemporaries and for many throughout history. It takes imagination to adapt and use this second foundation to launch us into the exercises of the Second Week. For example, we can—imaginatively—say that Ignatius is asking us to enter into Jesus' dreams for God's kingdom and our part in it. This exercise in itself is an engine of movement, which once again combines the elements of remembering and imagining, attracting us to Christ and so to his mission.

Finally, the Call of the King is imaginative in its reality as a foundation piece or a refining of the Principle and Foundation. The newness of this foundation is the person of Christ and his identification of his mission to proclaim the kingdom of heaven or reign of God. From our first foundation we are still in the context of God's continuing love, God's showering of gifts, and our effort to make the choices of response to God's love. Ignatius is careful in presenting his vision pieces—the Principle and Foundation, the Call of the King, and the Contemplation on the Love of God—to emphasize always the same vision, and yet each time with a further refinement or greater sense of completeness. It is the imaginative element in the presentation that triggers the movement toward the next stage of living our response to God more fully.

We enter into the contemplations proper to the Second Week, beginning with the Gospel's annunciation mystery, but placing it in the context of the Triune God who looks upon the world and chooses to enter into creation and heal it from within by being born a human being. We touched upon this scene when we were describing Ignatian contemplation earlier. The content matter of the second prayer period of the day is the biblical mystery of the nativity; it provides Ignatius with the opportunity to give a second explanation of how to enter into this form of contemplation.

Ignatius suggests a three-day period for our entering into this contemplative way of praying, our coming to appreciate the beginnings of Jesus' life, and our settling into a restful and quiet pace after the demands of the First Week. The director's imaginative adaptation to the retreatant either lengthens or shortens these first days of the Second Week.

The Ignatian-designated "fourth" day is a total change of pace, a return to the prayer of meditation for the whole day. We pray for the grace of understanding—understanding the deceits which the evil spirit uses to ensnare us and understanding the values that Jesus chooses for himself, and for us, to be able to live freely as the adult children God has called us to be. Using the meditative way of praying and asking for the grace of understanding would seem to suggest a very rational, thinking kind of day.

And yet Ignatius is particularly imaginative in presenting the meditative material of the day. He draws the picture of two opposing forces flying their own flag of allegiance. The place is here on earth: Jerusalem, a city whose name signifies the "peace of God," where Christ is the commander-in-chief of the good, and Babylon, a place whose biblical name is identified with noise and confusion and division among people, where Lucifer is the chief of the enemy. To whom is Lucifer enemy? Lucifer, whose name means "a bearer of light," is identified as the mortal enemy of human nature. The imagination used in small details by Ignatius shows up again in his choice of the verbs associated with Lucifer, such as "issues a summons," "scatters," and "cast out nets and chains." These verbs contrast with Jesus' "choosing," "sending," and "recommending . . . to want to help." Lucifer, seated on a great chair, is obscured by fire and smoke; Jesus stands on the level plain, to be seen with his followers. Lucifer tries to entrap through riches (and Ignatius qualifies this observation with, "as in most cases") and then through the honors that follow and finally through pride. By these three steps people are led to all other vices. Jesus holds up the seemingly obscure values of poverty, powerlessness, and humility. But by these three steps people are led to all other virtues. Ignatius has imaginatively chosen to emphasize three not-very-apparent values from Jesus' life in the Gospels in the face of three apparent worldly values that seem to be common across cultures and centuries. It is from this prayer exercise that Ignatius expects God's grace to enlighten the mind of the retreatant so as not to be deceived by Lucifer's values and to be able to guard against them. Our meditation will help us to understand Christ's choice of values so that we may imitate and follow him.

Although the final prayer period of this fourth day is uncharacteristically a meditation on new matter, Ignatius brings a certain lightness to it by employing our imagination. He makes use of a kind of case-study model to bridge the gap between understanding and action. By using this approach, he indicates that in objectively considering different groupings of people and how they face decisive action we have a method for eliciting our own subjective readiness to follow Christ in his chosen way of living.

The fifth day of the Second Week returns us to our contemplative way of praying. But Ignatius provides two more new exercises that draw us further into the use of our imagination. The first exercise has usually been given the title "Three Manners (Kinds, Degrees) of Humility." The second exercise deals with the Ignatian election—the matter to be considered in it, the times for making it, and the methods to be used. Even though the election plays its own essential role in the movement of the Second Week and in the director's sensing of its completion, I want to hold off our further study of it now and consider it later as a part of our treatment of discernment.

Humility, as we have experienced in the Two Standards meditation, is for Jesus the virtue of identity. Humility, living true to oneself, is Jesus living his truth—being true to his identity as Son of God. Ignatius proposes this exercise—it extends over a few days while we are entering into our prayer about the public life of Jesus—so that we may ruminate about how closely we image our identifying with Jesus. How much do we want the truth of Jesus' life to be embodied in our own? Remembering allows us to associate the second degree of humility with the Principle and Foundation consideration. To what excesses will we let love lead us? The picture that Ignatius paints of the third manner of humility is like a love song that speaks in metaphors of excess. One's pure rationality cannot understand this third manner; only a lover's imagination can begin to grasp it and let it become the dynamics of one's life. Ignatius suggests that, after a time of rumination on these manners of humility, the retreatant begin to pray for the grace of this identity or at least for the desire of such a grace.

The Ignatian election, which deals specifically with life choices or decision making about a reform of one's life, becomes another occasion to use one's imagination and not just one's rationality. Although both the election activity and the consideration of humility are to be done outside of the regular prayer periods, our sense that we have completed the Second Week or, as we might also say, our judgment that we have received the grace of the Week is readily made in terms of our response to the third manner of humility or to the resolution of our specific and embodied way of following Christ. How a Week is determined to be completed (since there is no set number of days) is a matter of imagination on the part of both the retreatant and the director. The retreatant is trying to report to the director where God's grace seems to have led, and the director is attempting to hear from the retreatant how the grace prayed for and the grace received come together to indicate future direction, if we want to follow God's lead. No *one* grace named can be identified as *the* gift of a Week of the Exercises. The continuing movement of the retreat flows from the imaginative interchange between the retreatant and the director.

C. The Third Week

Ignatius appears to be aware that our memory of the events of Jesus' passion and death can be an obstacle in the Third Week. He shows this awareness by his addition of three more points for each prayer period. Ordinarily the points of a prayer period serve to focus our attention on particular areas of the matter under consideration. When Ignatius presents the material for the events from the Last Supper through the burial of Jesus, he adds three points, all of which help us get inside the mystery and not just stay with external happenings. We pray for the grace that Christ will let us share his feelings as together we contemplate these days when he accomplished his greatest work, the work that his Father had given him to do, the work of redemption. Each of the added Ignatian points stresses this intimacy with Jesus. The grace of compassion is often described as the summary gift to be sought in the Third Week. Granted that the grace of God is most essential, the power of our imagining is what allows us to grow in compassion. We image ourselves being with others in their feelings, their joys and successes, their sorrows and failures. Compassion is the most precious of the graces in the Third Week because it signifies a wholly new intimacy and closeness to Christ. Just as the movement involved in our deepening relationship with Christ is quite different from the First Week to the Second, so too do we find a similar kind of movement in intimacy between the Second Week and the Third. The Third Week has little to build on if an appropriate Second Week grace has not been received. But the Third Week grace of intimate relationship with Jesus goes well beyond that of the Second Week.

D. The Fourth Week

In a similar way the Fourth Week has nothing on which to build if some Third Week grace of compassion has not been received. For in the Fourth Week Ignatius wants us to pray for the grace to let Christ enter us into his joy of victory. We may find it difficult to experience the consolation that the risen Jesus offers us. The world looks so much the same after his resurrection; we seem to struggle in many ways even though we have been baptized into Christ. How do we experience the risen Jesus and the power of his resurrection in our life? If we have known the precious gift of compassion in the previous Week, then we realize that in a similar way Christ stands with us in every life situation. Christ does not save us from life's trials; rather he supports us with his consoling power. Our experience of compassion is now reversed, inasmuch as we drink in the presence of our God of compassion and consolation—One with us, our Emmanuel.

Again Ignatius provides a way to realize this new relationship to God. In addition to the usual three points of a contemplation, he now adds two other points. Using these points, Ignatius draws our attention to the divinity shining out in the risen Jesus and to the role of consoler that identifies his way of acting. Throughout the usual contemplative prayer dealing with the mysteries of the risen life of Jesus, Ignatius adds this focus of a compassionate, consoling God. This emphasis provides a deepening relationship between God and us, sung, as it were, in a whole new key. The specialness of the deepened relationship is further clarified in the last structural piece of the Exercises.

The final exercise of the Fourth Week is titled The Contemplation to Attain the Love of God. Various commentators have pointed out that the four points of this contemplation roughly recall our experiences of the Four Weeks. That the matter of this last prayer is not new material allows for the prayer to be truly a contemplation. We can easily gaze upon what is now familiar to us. The newness comes from the imaginative way that Ignatius frames this prayer exercise. For the first time he offers two prenotes, rationally presented, coming from remembered human experience about loving. Building on the factual character of these prenotes, we see God pouring out love in such limitless ways that we are left gasping to make a response. The creativity of the colloquy response, originating with Ignatius, lies in its careful selection of what we can share of something we might be able to call our own.

Since we have imbibed from the Principle and Foundation that everything we have is gift from God, what then as lovers do we have to share with God except what he has already given to us? The "take and receive" of the Ignatian prayer response does not mean a "giving away" because we remember from Ignatius's prenote that lovers share what they have. So we humans can *share* with God our potential for making ourselves who we are—our liberty. We can share with God our memory because what we remember is truly ours—*our* memories—and so we can share it with God in love. We can share our understanding because what and how we understand is not quite like anyone else's way, and so we share this uniqueness with God. Finally, our will we share because our will signifies so much what we want, and so our wants and our choices we offer to God out of a sharing of love. This prayer is Ignatius's imaginative creation of how we share as a lover. He suggests that we can respond to each point of the contemplation in whatever way love moves us, and thus he offers his prayer response only as a model. He calls us to use our imagination to speak out what and how we as lovers can share with our loving God. The Ignatian prayer retains its classic popularity as a response because it has cut to the quick of imagining what we have to share with God. However we express our response, we are entering more fully into God's way of loving. From such pervasive contact with God, we are setting forth as contemplatives in action—this will be the movement of our life. We have made the Ignatian dynamics our own.

Truly the Ignatian Exercises do not have a closure or ending. The dynamics present in the retreat itself becomes the dynamics of human living in Christ. The interplay between remembering and imagining is the dynamics of the Exercises made visible to the retreatant. The dynamics of that interplay is what continues to empower and vitalize the person who lives an Ignatian spirituality.

Chapter Four

ADAPTATION FIRST

One of the peculiarities of the *Spiritual Exercises* book is that it does not start with a "chapter 1." Rather Ignatius begins with a section of directives for the proper use of the text. He entitles this part *Anotaciones,* literally "Annotations" but also translated simply as "Notes" or "Introductory Observations."

Ignatius makes clear that adaptation to the retreatant is central to all the directives that he gives. He emphasizes this dynamic adaptation, not by using some word meaning "adapt," but by placing first in the book the directions for adapting to a particular retreatant the Exercises that follow. Ignatius did not intend the Exercises to be made simply as they are written in the book; rather, for each retreatant, the Exercises can be given only as adapted and applied (the Spanish *aplicar* Ignatius does use once [18]).[1] It follows, then, that there is no such thing as "giving the pure Exercises," in the sense of using the Ignatian text literally as it is printed. Adaptation is key to the Ignatian dynamics.

By first emphasizing adaptation, Ignatius indicates that the one giving the Exercises (commonly in the tradition called the "director") has already made them, ordinarily once in their full form and perhaps also in a number of short retreats. From past personal experience of making the Exercises, the director knows how the retreat had been adapted specifically to him or her. By putting directions for adaptation first in the book, Ignatius is underscoring that the director must not think of his or her retreat experience as the paradigm for giving the Exercises. The Exercises retain their Ignatian character only if they are truly adapted and applied to each retreatant.

---

[1] Philip Endean, SJ, has emphasized Ignatius's use of the Spanish word *aplicar* (apply) in the Eighteenth Annotation and his nonuse of any Spanish word explicitly meaning *adapt*. See *Review of Ignatian Spirituality* (Rome: Centrum Ignatianum Spiritualitatis), 2002.

Adaptability of the Director

Ignatius presumes that we step forward as a director of the Exercises from an experiential knowledge of their full movement. Because we as directors have had the experience of making the Exercises in their Ninetieth or Twentieth Annotation form, we can more easily adapt any exercise to the one now making the retreat under our direction. How we adapt exercises to a particular retreatant is shaped, in part, by the full movement of the retreat or at least the movement within the Week taken as a whole.

In the Eleventh Annotation , Ignatius observed that the one who is receiving the Exercises (the one we commonly call the *retreatant*) is not to know in the First Week what he or she is to do in the Second Week. All the attention of the retreatant is focused on the matter at hand. At times in their conducting the retreat, it seems that directors take this note and apply it to themselves. For example, we directors know that the God of the Principle and Foundation is the same God we will see in the Contemplation on the Love of God. We need to be consistent when we present the image of God throughout the Exercises and especially when we prepare the points for each prayer exercise. In a later chapter, we will note how our relationship with God continues to deepen throughout the Exercises as we see different faces of God. But the consistency of our God image from the first exercise of the retreat through the last is very important. This consistency is the director's responsibility, and it can only be achieved if the director is experientially familiar with the whole movement of the Exercises.

The adaptations noted in the first twenty Annotations [1-20] of the Exercises set the tone for the progress of the retreat. Ignatius continues to remind the director with further notes, sometimes called *additions* (to what preceded, obviously), about accommodating the Exercises to the retreatant. These directions are greater in number throughout the First and Second Weeks than in the following Weeks. Ignatius seems to presume that the mutal sensitivity of the director and the retreatant has been developing during the first two Weeks so that fewer reminders about the accommodation of the subsequent Weeks' exercises need to be made as the retreat progresses. In fact, as we observed earlier when looking at the dynamics between the Weeks, Ignatius seems to give to the director, and through the director to the retreatant, a great freedom in the prayer exercises of the Third and Fourth Weeks, but always with a view to what is better for *this* retreatant.

Adaptability of the Exercises

Built into three of the first annotations [18, 19, 20] is Ignatius's acknowledgement that the Exercises, even in their basic formula, are meant to be accommodated. The Eighteenth Annotation has been receiving more attention in recent years, especially because of the widespread popularity of the Retreat in Everyday Life, identified with the Nineteenth Annotation. Since the Nineteenth Annotation (a Retreat in Everyday Life) and the Twentieth Annotation (the full thirty-day form of the Exercises), which is Ignatius's paradigm, are meant to have the equivalent dynamics, there is question whether many so-identified Nineteenth Annotation retreats today would not be more correctly directed after the manner of the Eighteenth Annotation (exercises accommodated to one who would not profit from the full movement). For example, Father Joseph Tetlow, SJ, has written a separate addition to his *Choosing Christ in the World*, an edition called *Lightworks*, mainly to present some simple exercises suggested by the Eighteenth Annotation.[2] Because some of the essentials of the full Exercises, such as the election and discernment processes, are possibly not integral to a retreat in everyday life as directed for a particular retreatant, a director needs to make deliberate choices about what adaptations are called for. Perhaps the ways of praying specific to the full Exercises may not fit the temperament of a given retreatant (not, say, a very reflective person) or, perhaps, the difficulty attending to affect may give a signal to the director to adapt the retreat as indicated in the Eighteenth Annotation. We have recently, then, re-discovered that the Retreat in Everyday Life frequently calls for adaptation according to the Eighteenth Annotation and not the Nineteenth Annotation.

The adaptation of the full thirty-day Exercises described in the Nineteenth Annotation is most evident in the retreatant's limited prayer times within each day and in the carefully planned progression of the Weeks of the retreat over an extended period of time, perhaps from six months to almost a year. A corollary adaptation is the reduction in the frequency of director-retreatant meetings to every week or two. But we take note that the Nineteenth Annotation retreat as sketched by Ignatius has the full dynamics that we identify with the Twentieth Annotation retreat.

---

[2] *Lightworks* is published both separately and as an appendix to the 1999 edition of *Choosing Christ in the World*. See p. 2 n. 4 above.

In describing the full Exercises of the thirty-day retreat in the Twentieth Annotation, Ignatius identifies its advantages in the naming of its various adaptations to personal situations. The basic adaptation is the retreatant's going apart from family and friends, from home, and from work. From that it follows that we are adapting our usual scattered attention to a single focus on God and the movements of God within us. Further, we are adapting our often-spontaneous choices to an awareness of our deepest desires and the freedom to choose in accordance with God's grace. Finally, we find ourselves adapting even our way of expressing our love of God, namely, to a new, focused intimacy of response. Since every Ignatian retreat demands adaptation, the full thirty-day Exercises makes the greatest demand on the sensitivity of the director to be continually aware of the movements of the spirits in the retreatant and adapting accordingly day by day.

Adaptability of the *Reglas*

Another signal that accommodations are to be made is given by Ignatius's various sets of *reglas* (guidelines or, literally, rules). Although we will consider the Ignatian *reglas* later, in chapter 16, we note here that what we commonly read as "rules" in translations of the Ignatian text is more accurately translated from the original Spanish or Latin texts as "guidelines," "measures," "norms," or "models." Ignatius is not setting down commands, orders, or canons; he is suggesting the idea of *guidelines* or *norms*, ways of measuring our behaviors or actions. Obviously, if Ignatius is giving us guidelines, then they ordinarily cannot be applied in ever instance as hard and fast demands, but need to be adapted to the individual and to the individual's life situation. The two sets of guidelines for discernment emphasize how Ignatius is aware of the accommodation necessary for coming to know the movement of the spirits in the different time frames represented by the First and Second Weeks. The guidelines for eating, for almsgiving, for thinking with the church—they all need to be viewed through the lens of adaptation. This was as true in Ignatius's day as it is in our own. In fact, when Ignatius wrote his *Constitutions of the Society of Jesus*, he himself wrote, and encouraged his fellow Jesuits to write, various "particular" *reglas* or guidelines that would help Jesuits carry out certain jobs or responsibilities. In a similar way, Ignatius seems to give the guidelines specific to the ministry of almsgiving as an example or model of how retreatants could write their own guidelines for whatever profession or ministry they might be engaged in. The guidelines' purpose has always been the enhancement of a continually deeper union with Jesus so that his values and actions can be mirrored every more faithfully in our own.

While today there are a number of self-help books adapting the Exercises to one's private retreat, Ignatius did not intend his book *Spiritual Exercises* to be used to self-direct one's own retreat. Rather the book is meant to help a director help a retreatant; its directives aid the one giving the retreat to wisely adapt the text according to how he or she perceives the graced relationship developing between God and the retreatant as it is expressed in the retreat conferences. Of course, God is truly the Director of the retreat, but there are also the one giving the Exercises and the one making them and Ignatius's text too—each plays an active part. From the beginning of the book to its close, Ignatius indicates that it is the director's adaptation of the text to the retreatant that is essential to giving the Ignatian Exercises properly. Integral, then, to the dynamism of the Exercises as they were intended by Ignatius is the director's ability to adapt and apply them.

Chapter Five

THE EXAMEN AND OTHER WAYS OF PRAYING

Although contemporary discussion continues about whether to consider the Principle and Foundation a part of the First Week or not, we might also question whether the examen material is what actually begins the First Week. Inasmuch as Ignatius indicates in the Fourth Annotation that the First Week deals with the consideration and contemplation of sin, the examen seems to be ignored as integral to the Week. We see clearly in the text that he gives *First Exercise* [45] as the title to a meditation which applies the three powers of the soul to the first, second, and third sins. Is this first exercise intended by Ignatius to be the beginning of the First Week?

Obviously we deal with both the Principle and Foundation and the examen material at the beginning of the retreat, whether they are explicitly identified as integral parts of the First Week proper or not. In a later chapter we will consider the Principle and Foundation in detail. But it is important to note now that, if a retreatant were to spend some time within the first few days considering the Principle and Foundation, Ignatius would also expect that in the daily conference with the director the retreatant would receive some instruction on the makeup of the examen. Since the whole retreat is itself a reflective process, Ignatius is concerned that the retreatant begins to grow in the kind of reflection that the examination process involves. Just as the first days of the Second Week are devoted to learning a special way to contemplate the Gospels, so in the initial days of the retreat we expect to grow in our understanding and practice of examination as a form of prayer.

It seems appropriate that we should take under consideration the prayer of examination first, just as Ignatius presents it. Then we will survey other ways of praying which Ignatius incorporates into the Exercises.

Examining

Although *examination* is a familiar word, as used in the traditional phrase *examination of conscience*, the word *examen* seems favored by Ignatius and its usage is associated with Ignatian spirituality. Ignatius indicates a number of examen periods in a retreat. Probably the most familiar form of an examen is the examination of conscience as a personal preparation for the sacrament of reconciliation or confession. In Ignatius's day, the examination of conscience was part of popular devotional life. Ignatius suggests that we make this examen in five steps: We are to begin with thanks to God for benefits received; then we ask for the grace to know our sins and be rid of them; next we review our life in terms of thoughts, words, and actions; we ask pardon of God for the sins we have committed; and finally we are to make a purpose of amendment with the help of God's grace. Ignatius emphasizes two essential parts of every kind of examen: (1) we are always to begin by expressing gratitude to God, and (2) we are to acknowledge, and seek the lead of, God's grace in any personal effort we make. For Ignatius, then, every kind of examen is a prayer exercise. Making one's examen is never simply taking account of oneself, never just talking to oneself before God, but is always having a conversation with God.

The kind of examen that precedes confession can also be adapted to serve as the examen regularly prayed in the ordinary life of the believer. The same five-step format can be used. Ignatius is not originating a prayer form new to the Roman Church tradition, but he is giving this reflective examen a new emphasis by recognizing it as a necessary part of our growing relationship with God in a day-to-day way.

What is more original is what Ignatius explains first in this examen material within the First Week—the particular and daily examen. He integrates this kind of daily examen with the prayer exercises of all the Weeks of the retreat. Outside of the retreat, this examen remains a daily practice of anyone living an Ignatian spirituality. In introducing the particular examen, Ignatius identifies three daily times with its practice. The first moment of our day, upon arising, we should recall what practice we have chosen to attend to because it will likely enhance or hinder our relationship with God. Then, after the midday meal and after the evening meal, we should enter into the examen prayer itself. We come before God, asking for what we want, which is the grace to see what we have done or what we have failed to do with regard to a particular virtue or fault which we have chosen for our focus, thus "particularizing" the point of our examen. Ignatius suggests making a written account of both the noon and evening examen, thereby keeping a sort of score that can be used for our own personal challenge from morning to evening, from day to day, and from week to week. The examen closes with our expressing our resolve to respond ever more faithfully to God's grace.

At the completion of every prayer exercise is another form of examen, which Ignatius originates, called the "examen of meditation" [77]. Ignatius suggests that, upon the completion of a prayer exercise, we take time, up to a quarter of an hour, to consider in the presence of God what has happened to us during this formal prayer period just completed. If our prayer seems to have gone poorly, we look for what may have caused that; if we can discover the cause, we ask pardon of God and we seek to correct it with God's grace. If our prayer seems to have gone well, we thank God and resolve to be faithful in the same way in the future. Again we remind ourselves, both when expressing our sorrow to God and when giving thanks to God, that this examen or review is its own kind of prayer exercise.

The examen exercise not explicitly identified by Ignatius is the one that the director of the retreat prays. The evidence for this examen is found in the practice of directors from Ignatius's time up till our own day. This examen is rooted in the annotations, especially those dealing with "the one who is giving the Exercises," especially the Fourteenth, Fifteenth, and Seventeenth Annotations. In the Fourteenth, Ignatius suggests that the director needs to be reflective about the way in which he supports the retreatant experiencing consolation. In the Fifteenth, the director is to examine whether he or she is, in fact, serving as a balance in the retreatant's decision-making process. In the Seventeenth Annotation, the director is to stay alert to whether the retreatant's movements are being expressed and whether the director is responding in helpful ways. Additional directions given throughout the individual Weeks continually remind the director to examine how well he or she is adapting the particular Week's exercises to the retreatant. To sum up, the essential elements to be assessed in the director's daily examen of the conduct of the retreat include being a good listener, being a helper, being a balance, and being a support. In addition, the director's daily and particular examen remains a part of keeping his or her own balance in the dynamics of the Ignatian retreat. We remind ourselves that the director's examen is a prayer in the presence of God, not just a psychological self-evaluation of listening skills.

The emphasis on the examen that we find throughout the Exercises reinforces the position that Ignatian spirituality is a reflective spirituality. If we were people who lived a spontaneous approach to life, not evaluating or learning from mistakes, we would not be apt candidates either for making the Exercises or for finding a source of life in Ignatian spirituality. The Socratic axiom that "the unreflective life is a life not worth living" becomes incarnate in the basic exercise undergirding Ignatian spirituality—what today we call the "consciousness examen" or the "awareness examen." It is the application of the daily and particular examen in our times. According to a tradition of the Society of Jesus, Ignatius asked only that a Jesuit be faithful to this examen prayer if no other prayer was possible *this* day because of sickness, busyness, or some other reason.

Besides the examen in its various forms, Ignatius employs various other kinds of prayer in the Exercises. Some of them he describes in the text, but more often he leaves to the director working with the retreatant the task of making understandable one or other way of praying. Although Ignatius is careful to distinguish the meditative type of prayer of the First Week from the contemplation which he describes in the Second Week, there are some times when the words *meditate* or *contemplate*—in all their various verbs, adjectives, and noun forms—are used by Ignatius with little or no distinction. At those times he seems to be more concerned about our praying reflectively than our using one specified form of reflective prayer or another. Let us now consider some of the different approaches to praying that Ignatius gives in the Exercises.

Considering

The prayer approach used in the exercise titled the Principle and Foundation is best described as a *consideration* or a *rumination*. Ignatius makes clear that all the formal prayer exercises of a retreat day—the four or five exercises usually called *meditations* or *contemplations*—are indeed exercises in prayer by including as an integral part of them a formal *colloquy*. The noun *colloquy* (Latin *colloquium*) is derived from the verb *colloqui*, meaning "to talk together." By drawing attention to this aspect of our prayer time, Ignatius reminds us that we spend a lot of time with another person sharing an experience and perhaps only intermittently or summarily talking about the experience. *Colloquy* is often the term we use to limit our definition of prayer. Ignatius makes the commonsense observation that we can spend a major part of our intimate time with another without saying a word. At the same time, by highlighting the integral role of colloquy in a formal prayer time, he reminds us that all prayer is communication—not just a time of pondering our own thoughts.

When we describe the Principle and Foundation as a kind of consideration or rumination, we are noting the fact that Ignatius does not identify it as a formal prayer period as such, that is, one which would always have its colloquy. He is encouraging the retreatant to ponder the Principle and Foundation as an expression of his or her faith in God, in God's creation, and in God's expectation of our human response. We can recall that the words *consideration* and *considering* derive their mental-activity meaning from the physical activity of stargazing (the meaning of the Latin *considerare*). Similarly we know that the word *rumination* is related to the action of a cow chewing on its cud (the meaning of the Latin *ruminari*). Rumination used in relation to human activity describes the way that people can go over a subject in the mind repeatedly and slowly. The Principle and Foundation requires this kind of human response described as ruminating and considering. Even without Ignatius's suggesting it, retreatants may find themselves talking with God about the matter under consideration. Perhaps the director can gently indicate that retreatants may find that they are inclined to talk with God as they ponder the Principle and Foundation matter. A kind of colloquy happens. Clearly at this point we see that consideration or rumination is another form of prayer exercise.

When we take up the Call of the King at the beginning of the Second Week, we find ourselves invited by Ignatius once again to consider or to ruminate on this material. Similar to the Principle and Foundation, the Call does not have a colloquy, which would identify it as a prayer exercise. But it differs from the Principle and Foundation in that it does have preludes, in particular, the prelude of asking for a grace—here the grace not to be deaf to Christ's call, but to be ready and eager to do what he wants. What appears colloquy like—the prayer expression of the generous people [98]—is presented only for our observation; Ignatius does not identify their response as *our* colloquy. It would be far too early in the retreat to expect such a response from a retreatant. Ignatius is now only planting a seed that will have time to germinate and grow in the retreat days that follow. The parable and its application to Christ is truly a passage for our considering or ruminating—twice within the day as Ignatius directs. Once again we as retreatants may be inclined to talk with God about our thinking, and the director may gently open the door to such a response in "pointing" the day's exercises. Then, however the communication with God is stimulated, this consideration or rumination becomes a prayer exercise.

Ignatius clearly identifies the Three Degrees of Humility as a consideration or rumination. He suggests that a retreatant consider the matter at various times from the Fifth Day of the Second Week on, outside of the regular four or five formal prayer periods. Only after considering the matter of the Three Degrees for some time is the retreatant encouraged by Ignatius to take his or her reflections to prayer. So the Three Degrees of Humility become identified as a prayer exercise when the conversation with God happens, just as we have indicated in the previous two examples of considering.

All the material that Ignatius would have us consider as part of the Election is to be approached by way of consideration or rumination. Ignatius suggests that the retreatant ponder the material carefully, outside of the ordinary prayer periods. There will come a time when the retreatant will be talking with God about the life decisions that result from the Election process. At this point, again, the consideration and rumination become clearly a prayer time.

Meditating

Sometimes Ignatius suggests a meditative style of praying: in the First Week (in the first two exercises); in the Fourth Day of the Second Week, both in the matter of the Two Standards (especially in the first two periods) and in the Three Classes (which is the fifth prayer period of the day); and in the First Method of Praying (described in the supplementary material at the end of the *Spiritual Exercises*). Ignatius inherits a style of praying called *meditation*, whose process is described by the medieval scholastic theologians in terms of the faculties of the soul—memory, understanding, and will. In this way of praying, it is important for us to bring to mind (memory) what the subject matter of our prayer is, then to work at probing its meaning for us (understanding), and finally to make some personal commitment (will) as our response. Our colloquy (always identified by Ignatius) entails our talking with God—at any one point or continuously—during this prayer exercise. We may sometimes get fixated on the movement from memory to understanding to will and then to colloquy as if our prayer activity is set in this chronological order. But such an approach would misunderstand the dynamics of praying. We need to keep reminding ourselves that colloquy or talking together with God is what happens spontaneously anytime within the entire period of the prayer exercise and deliberately but naturally, as Ignatius is careful to note, when we take our leave at the end of a prayer period.

Contemplating

The *contemplation* that Ignatius describes, beginning with the first exercise of the Second Week, is original enough that it has borne the identity of "Ignatian contemplation" in the tradition of Catholic spirituality. A much older tradition of *contemplation* refers to a simple "gazing on" and meant a kind of prayer that rested in the presence of God, free of thoughts and movements. Ignatius tied his notion of contemplation to the Scriptures, specifically to the New Testament by way of his own citations. As we have previously noted, Ignatius suggests two ways for us to enter into this kind of contemplative attitude toward God's word. Let us now consider these approaches to contemplation more closely.

In the first exercise of the Second Week, Ignatius suggests that we place ourselves alongside our Trinitarian God [102], that we see the scene as God does, and that we listen to what is being said as God hears it and observe what people do as God observes. But we are not only observers (the contemplative gazers); we are involved in the event before us as much as God is involved. Ignatius is bringing home to us that God is an active participant in our everyday events and that in our prayer God is inviting us to experience how involved he is. Our colloquy is our conversation with God about how we are involved with him. Hugo Rahner has called this style of prayer contemplation "from above," meaning our observing from God's stance, our identifying with God's perspective.[1]

In the second exercise of the Second Week, Ignatius offers us a different way to enter into this form of contemplation. Hugo Rahner has identified this second style as contemplation "from within," meaning our being actively part of the scene, at the ground-floor level. Ignatius suggests that we participate in the scene in the role of a servant. Later traditions allow us to identify with one of the persons in the scene, such as Peter or Zacchaeus or Martha or Mary. The presumption of Ignatius is that we are

---

[1] See Hugo Rahner, SJ, *Ignatius the Theologian*, trans. Michael Barry, SJ (London: Geoffrey Chapman, 1968), chap. 1:1-31.

integral to what is going on in the event. We are participating. Again our colloquy, our conversation, may be with any of the people who can in our Scripture passage help us come to know a response to God. Although in the Exercises Ignatius confines his references to the New Testament, it is easy enough to see how we can apply the Ignatian form of contemplation to various stories about the events of God's dealing with the people of both Testaments.

From the insights Ignatius shares about contemplation, we can see how this prayer form demands that we use our ability to image. Unless we can be free enough to let our imagining power roam, we will not easily enter into this kind of prayer. Without the freedom of our imagining power, no text or story will evoke anything in us beyond the physical settings and actions of the event denoted by the words. But if we begin to really see the people and the setting, if we actually hear their words, if we appreciate their facial expressions, their gestures, their evident fear or courage, we will be present to the event in God's time. The full imagining of a scene escapes a number of people. Some are poor in visual imaging, but they may "hear" the words spoken. Others cannot so much describe a scene as share a sense of or a feel for a Gospel incident. Regardless of the limitations of our imagining powers, in Ignatian contemplation the word of God becomes a living word for us. We are coming to know what it means to tell our own Gospel.

We all have had the experience of telling the story of being at the bedside of a dying "Aunt Martha," and while telling the story we feel a lump in our throat and the tears come just as if we were witnesses once again to the actual event. All of us have experienced the event of some ridiculous interchange between a teacher or a fellow worker and ourselves, and the event is so real in the retelling that tears of laughter roll down our cheeks as well as those to whom we relate the story. *That* kind of involvement is Ignatian contemplation. We might not feel ourselves to be very imaginative, and the Ignatian directions to see the people and to listen to what is being said, and then to watch their actions may seem very stilted and even cause us to feel frozen in our response. Yet everyone of us can tell a story, and in our day-to-day life we usually do. The action of contemplating and our telling a story seem to be the same kind of activity for Ignatius.

Our telling the story ordinarily speaks out not only the story and its meaning (as we "tell" it), but also its significance as we look to the future. It may give us insight into our own behavior, other people's interactions,

God's ways of acting, and so on. We tell stories not just to remember the past, but also to learn for the future. Telling stories is our way of imbibing and sharing wisdom. Ignatian contemplation is a wisdom way of praying, integrated with the process of discernment.[2]

Praying Prayers

Two more ways of praying are clearly identified by Ignatius. They are included by him in the Three Methods of Praying that he adds at the end of the book *Spiritual Exercises*. Concerned that a retreatant continue to exercise an active, everyday prayer life, Ignatius gives three examples of prayer that require no book resources, not even the Bible. We have already looked at the first method, which suggests taking a meditative approach to those matters of our faith readily familiar to us, such as the ten commandments, the seven deadly sins, and the powers of the soul. Whenever we pray a prayer that seeks a grace-helped understanding (doing so might keep us in our own head), Ignatius is careful to remind us of our need to talk with God—our need for colloquy time.

The second method of prayer that Ignatius outlines for the continuing prayer life of the retreatant after the time of retreat focuses on the individual words of familiar prayers. Just as in the first method, Ignatius does not claim that he is creating a new form of prayer previously unknown in our Christian tradition. The emphasis is not on understanding, but on meaning and comparisons, on relish and consolation. As Ignatius points out, a single word may take up the whole of our prayer time, and so we would close by praying the entire prayer. This prayer might be summed up in the word *dwelling*—a dwelling way of praying, imitative of the way that the Word "pitched his tent" (made his dwelling place) among us.

The third method of prayer described by Ignatius is a rhythmic style of praying. We may be already familiar with this style of praying through the longtime popularity of the "Jesus Prayer" of the Eastern Christian tradition. Ignatius focuses on the breathing in and the breathing out as a way to hold a word or phrase of a familiar common prayer—the content matter being the same as in the second method. Bringing together our breath of life with words evocative of the Source of life lies at the heart of this prayer of

---

[2] See David L. Fleming, SJ, "A Letter on Ignatian Prayer," *Ignis* 31, no. 1 (2002): 23-26.

rhythm. We might describe this prayer as a prayer of resonance—our whole being resonating with the movement of the spiritual world. The Jesuit poet Gerard Manley Hopkins images this kind of prayer of rhythm in his poem "The Blessed Virgin Mary Compared to the Air We Breathe." Obviously we do not speak of a colloquy in these last two methods of prayer since the very way of praying involves us in contact with God and the world of the Spirit.

Preparatory Praying and Repetition

Two further observations about prayer inspired by the Ignatian Exercises should be noted. At the beginning of each formal prayer exercise, Ignatius carefully directs our attention to a preparatory prayer. Subtly he reinforces our contact with God from the very start of a prayer time, no matter the form of prayer. Ignatius suggests both an exterior deportment of reverence that readies the whole of our bodily being and a prayer expression that reiterates our soul response, which is always grounded in the Principle and Foundation of our spiritual life. The content of the preparatory prayer always restates our desire to live out more faithfully our foundational relationship with God. We pray that God take to his praise and service all that we think, all that we desire, all that we do this day. Ignatius, then, brings to this preparatory prayer exercise something original—a dynamic movement which deepens our consistent attitude and availability to God.

The prayer exercises identified as a *repetition* and/or an *application of the senses* are Ignatian ways of praying, but both ways are dependent upon previous prayer periods and their respective methods of praying. As we have noted, the process of prayer repetition—most important for the Ignatian dynamics—is a subtle sifting and refining of previous prayer movements on the basis of consolation and desolation, of insight, and of the experience of "nothing happening." The Ignatian approach to an application of the senses seems to flow from the preceding repetitions and to reflect our total personal response (that is, being present with our whole being to the responses in prayer we note throughout the day) in this final prayer period. Neither repetition nor application of the senses can be put forward as an Ignatian way of praying independent of some preceding prayer periods. But Ignatius stresses these two ways of praying as a follow-through on previous prayer periods so that we truly listen to the language of God spoken within our very being.

Although Ignatius is not known for being novel in his teaching on prayer, he has provided through the Exercises a wealth of prayer creativity, a creativity central to their dynamics. As a true prayer master, he has left us ways to always be true disciples—true learners—of prayer.

Chapter Six

FACES OF GOD

I want to explore an important aspect of the Ignatian dynamics that seems to receive little attention. A long tradition has identified a grace, variously named, that is special to each Week of the Exercises. Just as we pray for a *particular* grace in each prayer exercise (an Ignatian prayer trait summed up in the Latin phrase *id quod volo*, meaning "that which I want or desire"), it would seem equally true to our experience if we were to identify the grace dynamics pervading any one Week and to symbolize it in a word or phrase for the fruit of that Week's movement.

But perhaps, instead of trying to identify a Week with a special grace, we may find a greater specificity in each Week of the Exercises if we consider the retreatant's relationship with God. If I were to try to sum up this relationship developing throughout the course of the Exercises, I would use the image of "seeing the faces of God." The different faces of God that we experience in the Ignatian Exercises often escape our notice. Let us consider more closely this developing relationship with God.

We are familiar with the metaphorical language we use to describe the interior disposition of a person—expressions such as "why such a long face?" "how bright eyed you look today!" or "you look like the cat that swallowed the canary." The person is the same, but we describe the person's face in those different ways to express the change that we feel is affecting our relationship. For example, how often have we heard: "When she wears that kind of a scowl, I always avoid her"; "I don't deal with him when he walks around all teary eyed"; "I keep quiet when he approaches me with that clenched jaw." How we see the face of someone can have a profound effect on the way we relate to that person. In our relating to God, we are affected by how we image God or, more concretely, how we see God's face.

Throughout the Exercises, Ignatius carefully directs our gaze to images of God that are meant to affect our relationship with our God. Ordinarily in the Ignatian contemplations our gaze is focused on the face of Jesus. We need to remember Jesus' words to Philip that "seeing me, you have seen the Father" (Jn 14:8-9). Jesus' face, then, gives us a unique way of seeing God and relating to God. It is not God who is changing; rather it is our relationship that changes because of how we respond to the different ways we "see" God. The progress of the retreat can be measured by the deepening of our relationship with God. Let us trace some of these faces of God that we come to know in the Exercises and that affect our relationship with him.

A God Who Gifts

Ignatius knows that we all bring a relationship with God into the retreat. What we "see" in the Principle and Foundation is the God we have come to know from our faith, but now know with the Ignatian emphasis on that God as the One who is creating us and interacting with us in giving us the gifts of creation. God wants us to be involved in his creative action. This is a God who not only loves us into existence in this showering of gifts, but also desires us to grow and come to an ever-greater knowledge and love of him through the gifts that mirror him in so many fragmentary ways. This God of loving gifts is not a God of do's and don'ts, but a God who calls us to exercise our responsibility towards appreciating and using these gifts to better love him and find the fullness of life with him forever. Our imaging of such a God of loving gifts may be helped by our experience of our own parents, of parents we have known or parents we ourselves have tried to be, and of friends dearly special to us.

The face of God may not be too clearly etched in our imagination, but we experience an open-faced God, a welcoming God, a God we can be "at home" with. Perhaps if we were to fill out the spare, philosophical language of the Ignatian Foundation text, we could rightly use the richer, evocative expression found in the Prologue of John's Gospel and know the "Word in whom all things are created." This is the God we "see," now limned by the language strokes of the Ignatian Principle and Foundation.

A Prodigal God

From our ruminating on the Principle and Foundation, we enter into a natural flow into the First Week with its exercises on sin. In the midst of our first meditative exercise, Ignatius asks that we imagine ourselves placed before Jesus on the cross as we pray. Why is our imaging of Jesus on the cross so important for this first exercise? Ignatius carefully identifies Jesus as our Creator—the same God as our gifting God of the Principle and Foundation, the Word of John's Prologue. Ignatius wants to make sure that we know and accept the continuity of our God—the God of the Principle and Foundation and the God of this First Week. How has God come from being Creator to making himself man and from eternal life to this human life in time? How has he come to die this awful death?

We have asked for the grace of shame and confusion in this first exercise. As God's gift, grace is not something we stir up in ourselves, and yet sometimes a kind of shame is easy enough for us to induce in ourselves or let others impose upon us. But what we are asking for is God's gift of shame and confusion, a grace given to us. In the Ignatian colloquy, we are talking to Jesus about our sharing in his shame and confusion while he hangs upon a cross and looks upon us and our world. Like Jesus, when we are observers only (that is, not perpetrators) of an act of human meanness or racial injustice, we can know the experience of feeling shame. We feel ashamed of our human behavior one toward another. We know what it is like to feel the surging wave of violence in a crowd of looters, and we are left confused by this kind of senseless, destructive action. Jesus, looking upon the hatred, the violence, perhaps the cold indifference of human beings beneath his cross, feels shame and confusion. As in the Good Friday lamentations, we hear him crying out, "My people, what have I done to you? Answer me." So, as we enter into Jesus' experience, we may find ourselves experiencing the graced gift of shame and confusion that we have prayed for.

Jesus' face allows us to see God's response to sin and evil. By God's grace, his response becomes our response. Knowing this face of God made visible in Jesus affects all the prayer exercises of the First Week. The fifth and final prayer period identified by Ignatius again specifies our prayer with Jesus. We cannot forget that this face of God in Jesus helps us to see the awfulness of sin—sin in which we too have a share.

Because in this first exercise we have entered into the shame and confusion of Jesus as he experiences evil and sin, we come to see the awfulness of sin and so to touch into God's response to the mystery of evil. In the second exercise we find ourselves looking at our own personal history of sin and asking for the grace of sorrow and even tears. What is the Ignatian progression here? The grace of shame and confusion is God's gift enabling us to enter into his response to sin; the grace of sorrow and tears is God's gift empowering us to feel our own response to our sinfulness. The God of loving gifts has been reemphasized, especially in the points of the second exercise, as a God who through others and through his creation provides and supports us, even as sinners [60], so as to increase our gratitude in the midst of our sorrow. Our gratitude to God only deepens now, as we gaze at a face of God—a God who can be shamed and confused by the human response we make as a part of the mystery of evil, but a God who looks ever upon us with mercy and forgiveness. Our relationship with the God of loving gifts seen in the Principle and Foundation is developing into a relationship with a God who is loving forgiveness and tender mercy. Through our prayer exercises of this First Week, we have come to know in our experience the prodigal Father of Jesus' parable. We see the face of a loving, forgiving God.

A God Who Beckons

When we enter into the prayer exercise of the Call of the King, we come before the face of the risen Jesus—Jesus as he is now. We see in him the face of forgiving love, just as the first apostles saw him and heard his words about forgiveness on that first Easter evening. In the scene Ignatius paints, we hear the invitation to be with him in his continuing mission for the reign of God. Ignatius stresses how Jesus issues the call "to be with" him and "to be with him in labors," so that in following him now we accompany him into life forever.

What is the face of God that we see here? It is the Jesus who steps forward and chooses us; it is the Jesus who wants us in his company. It is the Jesus who wants to share with us the responsibility of laboring for God's kingdom. Salvation is God's gift, and Jesus invites us to be participants in this saving work of God. God's mercy knows no bounds. We ourselves, the very ones needing mercy, are called to be the extensions of God's mercy. Jesus beckons us, and in his face we see, not an indifferent inviting glance, but a fiery determination that would leave the ninety-nine to search out the lost one.

We again feel the movement of a growing relationship. We see the face of God whose forgiving love wants us to play an integral part in God's redemptive action, to be busy with Christ about the Kingdom of God. God wants us to be involved in his saving action.

The rest of the Second Week exercises fills out this deepening relationship. We see this process in the continuing grace we seek in every contemplative exercise, the grace to know Jesus more intimately so that our love for him will grow and we might each be the ever-closer follower.

Through Jesus' face we see what it means to live and work as God's family. Just as in the Gospel story that tells of his family being outside the house where he is teaching, we too experience Jesus' sweeping gesture of pointing to us and saying, "These are my mother and my sisters and my brothers." When Jesus teaches us to pray, the expression "Our Father" sums up this developing relationship between God and us, and between us and others. "Our Father" takes on new and richer meaning. This is the face of the familial God—the God who delights to be with "the children of men."

A God Who Is Love Crucified

We enter into the Third Week through our contemplation of the events surrounding the Last Supper. Although all the points for prayer form one unit, Ignatius focuses us on his third point where Jesus institutes the Eucharist as "the greatest mark of his love" [289]. By directing our attention to the face of Jesus as he invites us to take and eat—"This is my Body broken for you; this is my Blood poured out for you"—Ignatius points the way for us to come into the mysteries of the passion and death of Jesus. In giving us himself in the Eucharist, Jesus presents us with the key to understand and enter into his greatest work, the work of redemption. Ignatius is aware that, because the crucifix has been the central symbol of our faith and there are many devotions that emphasize the pain of the passion, such as the Stations of the Cross, we may be inclined to stay with the externals of the suffering and bloodshed. Ignatius adds three more points for our making all the prayer exercises during the Third Week, starting from the first contemplation. As we have noted in a previous chapter, each of the added points directs our attention to the interior of Jesus. We are begging Jesus to let us be with him "inside" the experience.

The very added points of our prayer betray the developing relationship of intimacy or interiority with Jesus. This is reinforced in the grace we pray for. We pray for sorrow (an affect response common to the second exercise of the First Week) and for confusion (an affect response common to the first exercise of the First Week), and, in general, for the deep feelings of involvement. The grief, the confusion, the heart-wrenching affect are aspects of the graced gift of compassion which distinguishes our response of this Week. Shame (a grace of the First Week) has no part in this Third Week grace since our focus is not fixed on ourselves or on our human failings, but looks only to our empathy with a God who does not hold back from gifting us even with his very Self. Our graced compassion becomes our way of reciprocating the love of God poured out so lavishly.

Jesus in his passion shows us a face of God that sets no limits—not even death, no matter how unjust or violent—to the ways he wants to share himself with us. Eucharist says it all: "Live in me, and I will live in you."

A God Who Knows No Limits

The Fourth Week begins with a first exercise, but no first day is identified. Following good theological tradition, Ignatius observes in such a subtle way that in the dying and rising of Jesus we move outside our ordinary time categories. In addition, Ignatius suggests for our first contemplation the appearance of Jesus to his mother, an apparition not recorded in the Gospels. Ignatius has more than a devotional exercise in mind when he begins the Fourth Week with the appearance of Jesus to Mary. The risen Jesus (the Ignatian use of the words *body* and *soul* to emphasize the whole reality of a human person) shows his face first to his mother. She sees the familiar face of Jesus, yet now different, and she realizes a new relationship with him. Mary, above all others, has had a unique intimacy with Jesus. From her extraordinary pregnancy through her giving birth and nurturing, Mary can look upon Jesus as her "heart enfleshed" walking around. They share the intimacy of mother and child. But now when he appears first to Mary, Jesus shares with her a far greater intimacy in that as the risen Jesus he truly penetrates her very being. The sharing of his risen life, which unites him with his mother, is the first joy of Jesus in his role as consoler. The grace we ask is that Jesus help us also to enter into this kind of joy.

We remember throughout the Fourth Week that Ignatius adds two more points to the usual three points of a prayer exercise. The added points, like the three added in the Third Week exercises, emphasize our effort to get inside the experience of the risen Jesus. Getting inside the experience of the risen Jesus with his mother Mary is the key to our gaining admittance into all the other resurrection appearances that make up the Week. The way Mary experiences the presence of her risen Son brings us to an appreciation of a wholly new way of relating that Jesus rejoices to share with us. Just as we saw in the Third Week a God who held nothing back and set no limits to the love he poured out, so also we see in the Fourth Week a God who rejoices in sharing his life with us now, a divine life where God has broken down all limits of intimacy. If in the Third Week we have been graced with compassion in our relationship to Jesus, we are ready now to be graced with the consolation of the risen Jesus in his victory over death (and every limit) in all its forms.

Just as our compassion did not change the historical fact of Jesus' death but did change us in our relationship, so too Jesus' consoling presence and action do not change the historical circumstances of our life but do affect our relationship to God and to our world. We see the face of God intimately close to us, our strength and consolation, our joy. Our life is already "hidden now with Christ in God" (Col 3:3).

A God Who Communicates

The final exercise of the Ignatian retreat is the Contemplation on the Love of God. The grace we pray for is the grace to be able to love the way that God loves. Ignatius situates this prayer exercise in the context of a prenote with two points about love. He notes that love is shown more in deeds than in words. Then he notes that love is all about communication, about sharing with the beloved whatever one has. Since Ignatius has carefully identified this exercise as a contemplation, it seems to me that the more fitting interpretation, alluded to in early commentaries and emphasized in contemporary ones, is to understand the four points of the exercise as a review of the experiences of the Four Weeks.[1] Each point allows us to think back over each Week and remember the face of God that we saw in each and how our relationship developed through that Week.

But Ignatius is presenting more than a retrospective exercise. In the points of his prenote, Ignatius is stressing how we can immerse ourselves in the vision of a God who is forever communicating with us, and how his message and his action are always the same revelation: "You are my beloved." The words that Jesus heard at his baptism and at his transfiguration are the words that God continues to speak to us. The face of God is of One who loves us and never stops acting out his love. Ignatius then calls for our response. If we see such a face of God, what kind of face do we show to God and to our world, God's world?

---

[1] See Martin Palmer, SJ, trans. and ed., *On Giving the Spiritual Exercises: The Early Jesuit Manuscript Directories and the Official Directory of 1599* (St. Louis: Institute of Jesuit Sources, 1996).

Let us end where we began. We are familiar with the many faces that a person we love can share with us. Those faces call forth from us various responses. In a similar way, we can grow in response to the way that we see various faces of God. Each face calls forth a different response from us. God is always the same God, but in our various experiences we can see different divine faces. The faces that Ignatius has given us to see, especially through Jesus, have helped us grow in our relationship with God. Throughout our life we will continue to see faces of God, and we will continue to grow in our relationship with God. That is a dynamic, lasting gift of the Exercises.

Chapter Seven

THE FOUNDATIONS

The Principle and Foundation is the first exercise of the Ignatian retreat. Its very title bluntly states its place in the Exercises. Ignatius wants to ensure that the director and the retreatant agree on a basic *ground*work of faith—to use the "foundation" image—on which the retreat can build or from which it can move upward. Since we are considering the *dynamics* of the Exercises, perhaps our imagery is more fitting when we speak of the first exercise as the Principle (from the Latin *principium,* meaning *beginning* or *source*) because this exercise acts as the spring-source from which all the movements of the later exercises flow.

Just as we have been familiar with the idea that the Exercises move forward only after some time has been spent on the Principle and Foundation, so there is a long tradition identifying the exercise known as the "Call of the King" as a second foundation. It specifies the first foundation explicitly found within the Gospel context of every Christian's vocation.

A Principle and Foundation for Each Week

In addition to these two traditional foundations, I am proposing that we can find Ignatius developing a kind of foundational exercise proper to each Week. There are the two exercises which we identify as bookends: the Principle and Foundation at the beginning of the Exercises and the Contemplation on Love at their close. Regardless of how far we advance in the spiritual life, a solid grounding—the "house being built on rock" in Jesus' image—maintains its importance. We can never ignore our need to draw upon the richness of the Principle and Foundation as the beginning of an Ignatian retreat. In a similar way, the Contemplation on the Love of God, which is considered the final exercise of the retreat, acts as the foundation for our ordinary life after the retreat. It is a foundational exercise from which we draw consolation for our daily life because we need always the empowerment that we find in this exercise if we are to love in the way God loves. There is, then, a foundational exercise at the beginning and another one at the end of the Ignatian retreat. Both exercises are foundational, and at the same time they remain principle like, that is, animating in the manner of Ignatius's imagery of sun and spring-source in the fourth point of the Contemplation on Love.

Besides these bookend foundations for the Ignatian Exercises, I want to identify the first exercise as foundational for the First Week. Then I will look again at how the consideration of the Call of the King is foundational for the Second Week, and move on to examine how the Last Supper contemplation is foundational for the Third Week, and how the contemplation on the appearance of the risen Jesus to his mother Mary is foundational for the Fourth Week. We have seen in all four of these prayer exercises how Ignatius helps our God relationship grow by inviting us to respond to the images or faces of God which he points out to us in each of these exercises. But now our focus is on the way Ignatius has us ground all the subsequent exercises of a particular Week upon this new foundational exercise. Besides the imagery of grounding, we may also use the spring-source image since it allows us to appreciate how all the prayer exercises properly "flow" from our praying this first exercise in each Week. Let us look more closely at each of the identified foundational exercises.

The First Week Foundation

Ignatius presents the first exercise of the First Week as a meditation on sin objectively considered. We examine the one sin of the angels, the original sin of Adam and Eve, and the single sin of a person rejecting God forever. Ignatius intends for us to come to an appreciation of the awfulness of sin, not from the weight of numbers or from its pervasiveness, but from its very nature in a single act. We have noted that he does not have us pray for an *understanding* of sin since sin remains a central part of the *mystery* of evil. But Ignatius directs that we pray for shame and confusion, which we might suspect at first glance to be Ignatius's effort to have us feel bad and become introspective and self-focused. Yet since we are looking at the sin of others (our own sinful actions will be reviewed in the second exercise), our response is not subjectively motivated. By suggesting we take an imaginative approach to the colloquy—picturing ourselves present to Jesus, our Creator, as he hangs upon the cross—Ignatius sets the scene for our conversation, the conversation between Jesus and us. The questions that Ignatius proposes—What have I done for Christ? What am I doing for Christ? What ought I to do for Christ?—are not accusatory questions, demanding a confession-like response. Rather, the grace we seek (the second prelude) and our conversation with Christ on the cross (the colloquy) fit together as a coherent unit. Before these questions are posed to us, we wonder with Christ how he, being Creator of all, enjoying eternal life, has come to this end, for us sinners.

As we enter into conversation with Jesus on the cross, we are seeing and hearing and feeling Jesus' response to the sin and evil before him. In his love for us, which by our faith we have learned is what truly nails him to the cross, he is the first to feel ashamed of our human behavior and he is the one who is left confused by hatred and rejection of his love. In our conversation, Jesus shares with us this grace of shame and confusion. We are being gifted to see and respond to evil and sin the way God sees and responds to evil and sin. This exercise, then, situates us with God, and God graces us with the Christian response—the Christ response—to sin.

Now that Jesus has allowed us to share his response, we can look at our own history of sin and evil. The grace of shame and confusion assumes a new shape as a grace of our personal sorrow and, perhaps, even tears from recognizing our part in the continuing rejection of the One who continues to love us and shower us with gifts. The rest of this first day, as well as the rest of the Week, flows from the spring-source of the first exercise. When we enter the First Week through the door of its own foundational exercise, then the introspective, breast-beating kind of behavior that is sometimes associated with the "Week on sin" is less likely to become our focus. Surely the feelings of sadness, the sense of being in darkness, and the weight of the petty meanness of our life are part of personal responses that naturally fill out the grace of shame and confusion. But throughout the Week constantly Ignatius keeps our eyes on God and Jesus. We find ourselves continually saying "thanks" to a God who ever loves and gifts and forgives. Even in the face of a hell that the weight of sin impresses upon us—the fifth and final exercise of the day—we still look, by Ignatius's own directions, only with gratitude to Jesus as our saving and forgiving God.

The Second Week Foundation

The exercise Call of the King has traditionally been identified as foundational, not only to the Second Week, but to all the following Weeks, which also focus on Christ. Ignatius has identified this exercise as a "help" toward contemplating the life of Christ. What is striking about the exercise is the objective approach that Ignatius employs. Not only does he begin with the parable story of a king and his call, but he also makes the comparison to the risen Christ, who is still calling out to everyone to be his follower. In the second prelude of the exercise, we are asking for the grace not to be deaf to Christ's call, but to be ready and eager to do what he desires. The seeking of grace is the subjective aspect of the exercise. While in most exercises of the retreat the director assesses the movement of the particular exercise by listening carefully to what grace the retreatant prays for in the prelude and then to what in the conversation or colloquy time the retreatant and God talk about, here in the Call of the King exercise there is only the prelude and no colloquy is suggested. Instead of the subjective interactive response that makes up the colloquy, Ignatius would have us listen to the objective response of the magnanimous and generous person. We find ourselves inspired, we are being given a good model, and we hear the prayer of the person on fire to serve. As retreatants, we are truly disciples, "student learners," and so we may not be able at this time to speak out meaningfully such a generous spiritual response as we hear from others in this third point [98]. But Ignatius has planted the seed (and we have asked for that grace), and now we want to observe Jesus carefully so that we might come to really know him and drink in all that it means for us to make our response by following him. In this way, the Call of the King exercise is the spring-source exercise from which flows our wanting to know Christ Jesus in the exercises of the Second Week that follow.

While the Call of the King exercise does look forward to the rest of the Week, it also has a way of looking back toward the First Week. Jesus invites us all, in a way that is very particular and unique to each person, to have a part in his saving mission. If we felt ourselves the recipients of Jesus' saving action in the First Week, now we hear ourselves invited to "be with" Jesus and to "work with" Jesus. Jesus wants us to play an integral role with him in the saving action of God. The exercise Call of the King, then, finishes the First Week as a true expression of God's mercy. God is not content with doing something for us, but seeks to involve us in his merciful action. God's mercy is experienced in his desire to have us work with him in bringing about the Kingdom.

We are changing our imagery when we describe the Call of the King exercise as a "bridge" prayer period between the First Week and the Second Week. It can truly be said to complete the First Week inasmuch as Christ's seeking us out and calling to us is reminiscent of the father running out to greet his prodigal son in Jesus' parable. The call to be Christ's disciple incarnates God's mercy. We resonate with Peter's response to Christ's call: "Leave me, Lord, for I am a sinful man" (Lk 5:8). When we consider the same prayer exercise as directing us towards the Second Week, it leads us perhaps even more obviously to pray the Gospel mysteries with the clear intention of coming to know God as the One who is calling and who seeks our love and following.

The Third Week Foundation

The Third Week begins with the contemplation of the events surrounding the Last Supper. We may consider it the first day only insofar as it is the chronological beginning of the passion events. But Ignatius is careful in his *pointing* of (that is, giving points for) this prayer exercise [289]. The first point presents Jesus and the apostles eating the paschal lamb meal, with all its ritual meaning. The second point dwells on Jesus' washing of the disciples' feet as the summary example of how we should act as Jesus has acted. The third point focuses on Jesus instituting the "sacred sacrifice of the Eucharist, to be the greatest mark of his love." Although each point is significant for our entering into the mystery, the language that Ignatius carefully chooses in this third point—"to be the greatest mark of his love"— becomes the key to our entering into all the mysteries of the passion and death of Jesus.

The Last Supper ritual and especially the institution of the Eucharist are the spring-source for our entering into all the mysteries of the Third Week. Our eyes and our heart take in all the sufferings and pain that Jesus endures, but they are not stopped by these horrendous happenings. When we observe the three added points that Ignatius proposes for all the exercises of this Week, we find ourselves always seeking to be invited into the interior experiences of Jesus in every prayer exercise. The Eucharist is the key, the source, of this way of intimacy with Jesus. The Last Supper and Eucharist, mysteries though they be, allow us to enter fully into the mystery of Christ's passion and death. Eucharist is where Jesus is; Eucharist is what gives everything that happens to him purpose and meaning. We are caught up in a love that holds nothing back, a love that accepts even death—seeing death, in faith, as no limit to God's love. The Last Supper and Eucharist, then, become the spring-source for our graced response of compassion throughout the contemplations of the passion.

The Fourth Week Foundation

The Fourth Week begins with a slight anomaly in that Ignatius does not identify a first day. Rather, the flow that he indicates in the last exercise of the Third Week—describing the late Good Friday burial of the dead body of Jesus, and the Holy Saturday activities of Jesus as his soul goes to the realm of the dead to announce the Gospel, and then his being raised, body and soul, at the beginning exercise of the Fourth Week—is not measurable in days. We have entered into the resurrection life, and our time measurements do not apply. And so the Fourth Week truly does not have a first day, but it does have a first exercise.

The first exercise, described as the appearance of the risen Jesus to his mother Mary, is often taken as an exercise of merely pious value because, of course, it has no scriptural foundation. Though the prayer exercise may have no foundation in the Gospels, the exercise serves as a foundation for all the prayer exercises that follow. Inasmuch as Ignatius presents this exercise first, he intends it to be the key or source of our ability to enter into all the contemplations on the risen life of Jesus.

Mary as mother has had a most intimate relation with Jesus. She knew him not only in pregnancy, in birth, in nursing, and in rearing, but also in her love and support of his mission, all the way to the cross. When the risen Jesus—the whole composite of body and soul that Mary knew—appears first to his mother, she becomes the first to know the joy and consolation of a relationship with Jesus at a depth unimaginable. The risen Jesus penetrates the whole being of Mary. Mary, the first disciple of the risen One, becomes our teacher, showing us a depth of relationship with Jesus that we could never imagine—even as we have contemplated his life and ministry in the Second Week and as we have contemplated his passion and death in the Third Week. This foundational exercise points the way for us to understand how Jesus breaks through into a wholly new depth of relationship with Mary Magdalen, with Peter, with Thomas, and with all those to whom he appears, as we contemplate the various resurrection appearances. We are beyond our Second Week prayer of knowing him more intimately in order to love and follow and beyond our Third Week prayer of being compassionately present.

We note that the Annunciation contemplation, identified by Ignatius as the first exercise of the first day of the Second Week, introduces us through Mary's encounter with the archangel Gabriel to a new unimaginable way of "God being with us," namely, in the incarnation of the Son of God. Here in the first contemplation of the Fourth Week we have a new "annunciation" scene. Again, through Mary, we experience a wholly new depth of "God being with us" as Jesus, the risen Lord, presents himself to us.

If we understand the first exercise as foundational, we realize that in this Fourth Week God is inviting us into the mystical depth of relationship that the risen Jesus represents. Perhaps Ignatius is giving us a way to enter into the "not knowing," the "not recognizing," that flows through the various resurrection appearances. The risen Jesus is the same Jesus, but our relationship with him has so drastically changed that it is as if we had never really known him. This is why the grace we pray for in this Week is to let Christ help us enter into his joy and to know his consolation. When we are contemplating Mary and the risen Jesus, we are at the spring-source of experiencing the new depth of relationship that the risen Jesus continues to offer to all his followers.

The Foundation for Everyday Life

The Contemplation on the Love of God takes its place as the foundation for everyday life after the retreat inasmuch as it is a natural outflow from our contemplating the appearances of the risen Jesus. We easily see now how God's love has been communicated through all our prayer content of the Weeks of the retreat. But in light of the resurrection, we appreciate the depth and extent of God's ways of loving all the more. Our prayer is that God might enable us to communicate our love in the ways and to the depth that God does. We want, at the spring-source of our life, the grace to communicate love the way that God does.

As we look carefully at the Exercises, then, we see six foundational exercises employed by Ignatius. Each exercise is more than foundational, that is, providing the solid rock on which to build. Each exercise is a spring-source that provides the flow for all the exercises that follow. These six basic exercises contain the dynamism that provides the foundations and the spring-sources of our life in Christ.

PART II

MAKING CONNECTIONS

Chapter Eight

BEGINNINGS: SEEKING GOD AND FINDING GOD

In the language of Ignatian spirituality, who is the God whom we struggle "to seek and to find" in our everyday life? Ignatius has us begin with the God imaged in the Principle and Foundation. Which face of God do we see in this opening prayer reflection?

Since we have a certain familiarity with the concepts of the Principle and Foundation, are perhaps even bored by its factual presentation, we say that we are being presented with a creator God. Maybe we do not find a creator God to present much of a face; perhaps we see an almost abstract, philosophical God. But, if we make a closer inspection, we find Ignatius emphasizing that we can see not only a God who loves us into existence (that is, gifts us with creation), but also One who continues to give gifts—in fact, surrounds us with gifts so that we might come to know and love and respond to this God. We can see a God who bids us choose from among the gifts given us, on the basis of how much these gifts help us "to seek and to find" God. *That* is one way of summarizing the Ignatian Principle and Foundation.

Only One God

We might note that Ignatius does not use the word *love* in the text of the Principle and Foundation. What is more important, however, is the fact that *we* bring to the Ignatian paragraph our biblical notion of a God of love. Since we know that Ignatius has a closing prayer exercise titled "Contemplation on the Love of God," we are aware that the continuity of the face of God from the beginning of the Ignatian Exercises until the end is that of a loving God. The director of the retreat is not presenting two conflicting Gods—one who is indifferent and withdrawn and one who is involved and loving. As retreatants we do not approach the Principle and Foundation with a blank, inquiring, philosophical mind. We bring our faith and our experience of God. God creates because he loves.

What is our principal and foundational image of God—the one with which we are always meant to live? God is the name we give to a relational

Being. It is the Christian belief that our Trinitarian God is a God identified as Love. In St. John's blunt words, "God is Love." But perhaps even that scriptural statement sounds too abstract or too static. Maybe we might better say, God is Love loving. For we observe in Ignatius's picture of God given in the Principle and Foundation, our God is a God who is actively gifting us—Love loving. Looking further at St. John's description, "God first loves us and then . . . ," we note that *then* indicates that our response follows. God loves, and so God creates, God gifts, and God continues to gift. We see that God's love is not something we earn or buy, wheedle or plead for. God's love is first, is a given, and is seen to be "unconditional."

Although some contemporary translations of Scripture can slip up in their inadequate choices of translation and lead us astray, as a matter of fact we do not find in Scripture God saying, *if* you do such and such, I will love you.[1] God does not say: I will love you *only if* you kill your firstborn; I will love you *only if* you go to Lourdes; or I will love you *only if* you keep my commandments. God is always Love loving or a Giver gifting. *That* truly is the image that Ignatius is checking to see if we are feeling at home with as we enter into a retreat. *That* is our foundational image of God.

Because we believe in a God of love, "unconditional love," *therefore* it follows that the choices that we make in life are, deep down, all about our seeking and finding the Giver of these gifts that reflect him. If some gifts seem to lead us away from God, no matter how good the gift, we decide that these gifts are not helpful to us and so we turn away from them. Ignatius seems to indicate that our behavior follows upon our grasping that God loves us into existence and seeks our cooperation in our growth and fullness of life. God loves us from the beginning, with no conditions imposed on us. Knowing that we are God's beloved, we desire to behave and act in ways like God, the one who loves us into existence. There is a great difference between seeing the face of a God who loves us *only on condition* that we do or act in such a way and seeing the face of a God who loves us unconditionally and *as a consequence* we want to act—to respond—in a loving way.

---

[1] I have been influenced in my approach by Antony F. Campbell, SJ, in his book *God First Loved Us: The Challenge of Accepting Unconditional Love* (New York: Paulist Press, 2000).

A Gospel Application

Perhaps we can better appreciate the Ignatian dynamics involved in the Principle and Foundation when we consider the passage in the Gospel of St. Mark (10:17-27) about the young man seeking out Jesus.

As [Jesus] was setting out on a journey a man came running up, knelt down before him and asked, "Good Teacher, what must I do to share in everlasting life?" Jesus answered, "Why do you call me good? No one is good but God alone. You know the commandments: You shall not kill; You shall not commit adultery; You shall not steal; You shall not bear false witness; You shall not defraud; Honor your father and your mother." He replied, "Teacher, I have kept all these since my childhood." Then Jesus looked at him with love and told him, "There is one thing more you must do. Go and sell what you have and give to the poor; you will then have treasure in heaven. After that, come and follow me." At these words the man's face fell. He went away sad, for he had many possessions. Jesus looked around and said to his disciples, "How hard it is for the rich to enter the kingdom of God!" The disciples could only marvel at his words. So Jesus repeated what he had said: "My sons, how hard it is to enter the kingdom of God! It is easier for a camel to pass through a needle's eye than for a rich man to enter the kingdom of God."

We note that, for this person, seeking eternal life or God is a matter of "doing." He seems to say, "I want to do these things so that I can gain God's love." When Jesus reviews those commandments dealing with our ways of acting towards others (acting the way God acts), the man sounds disappointed. Maybe he was expecting Jesus to say he needed to fast on all Wednesdays and Fridays or maybe that he should observe the nine First Fridays and the five First Saturdays—anything he could *do* so that he could have God in his debt. He would be earning God's love, gaining eternal life.

Jesus sees his good will and looks upon him with love—God's love. The man did not earn it or work for it; Jesus just loves him. And so Jesus invites him to a whole new way of understanding a relationship. Jesus puts it in terms of *doing*, but all the actions are in terms of *letting go*. Selling and giving to the poor and following. There is much more here of *un-doing*, of giving up control, of letting ourselves be taken. Jesus is trying to teach this man about a relationship with him (Jesus) and so something about our relationship with God.

When the disciples reflect that this idea sure sounds hard—because what we do *is* our riches, we get what we earn, we want to be in control—Jesus agrees and says that it is well nigh impossible for us humans. But with God's grace—another gifting which leads us on—we then find it possible. God's first loving us is what makes everything we do possible.

When we truly drink in deeply that God loves us now, as we are, then we realize that our life is not a time of testing. Lovers do not test. Our life is a time of growing and maturing. As St. Paul describes it, it goes from using a baby formula to eventually eating solid food—maturing in Christ. We are growing in our responsibility to make choices as God's loved ones.

Love's Environment

When we live in God's unconditional love, this world is hardly a valley of tears. Rather we see it as a world of God's gifting. But God's loved creation does cry out for us to act with God to bring it to a fulfillment and so to bring about the "kingdom of God," a reign of justice and love. God entered into his creation in a definitive way in Jesus Christ—as Ignatius helps us to realize. With the defining life, death, and resurrection of Jesus, God has entered all of us into the assured victorious struggle against every limiting factor, physical, psychological, and spiritual.

All of this way of thinking is included in the words of the Principle and Foundation. We are seeing the face of our Christian God—a Trinitarian God who is "altogether Gift," as a contemporary author, Michael Downey, describes our Trinitarian God.[2] God, the one we call Father, is the Giver; the Son is the Given; and the Holy Spirit is the Gift and Gifting. This God is the God of unconditional Love—the face of God most basic to our living life; this is the One we seek and the One we find. God as "Love loving" is truly our principle and foundation.

---

[2] See Michael Downey, *Altogether Gift: A Trinitarian Spirituality* (Maryknoll: Orbis, 2000).

Chapter Nine

THE FIRST WEEK: IMAGINING SALVATION

Ignatius in the First Week exercises is guiding us into various ways we can imagine salvation. How do we image or imagine salvation?[1]

Prenotes

The first prenote to this consideration of salvation is this: Ignatius presumes that every director of the Exercises has had the experience of being the retreatant in the thirty-day retreat. We made note of this in chapter 4 when dealing with adaptation. The director, then, is not approaching each Week of the retreat as its own separate unit—acting as if he or she does not know what is coming next. The director knows the flow of the movement from Week to Week, is aware of the importance of the unifying elements, and is able to direct and adapt each exercise accordingly. We sometimes approach a study of the text of the Exercises, or even enter into the direction of a retreat, without letting the flow and interaction of elements help us understand more deeply the makeup of the retreat and so direct more surely the one making the retreat.

We know that Ignatius's Eleventh Annotation deals with the counsel that the retreatant is not to know anything of what is to happen in the later Weeks lest such knowledge hinder the effect of what is going on in the current Week. As we have noted in chapter 4, we as directors sometimes seem to take this annotation as a guide for our own behavior. Yet we as directors need to bring the whole of our knowledge of the Exercises to bear on any element and its implications whenever it first appears. Our full knowledge is meant to help us, both as to what to say in direction and what

---

[1] The ideas in this chapter, which deals with the First Week, were first presented at the annual assembly of the U.S. Jesuit Retreat and Renewal Ministries Conference held at Campion Center in Weston, Massachusetts, in April 2001. A brief article, "Seeing the Face of God," was published in *Harvest* 34, no. 2 (Summer 2001): 6-7. A more developed presentation, "Seeing the Face of God: The First Week in the Ignatian Exercises," was published in *Ignis* 31, no. 1 (2002): 18-21.

not to say—all with a view to how we can be helpful to the retreatant and the better progress of the retreat.

For example, when we are directing someone in the First Week, we can appreciate how we draw upon our familiarity with certain key elements flowing through all the Weeks of the retreat in order to make a better presentation of the matter when the element makes its first appearance. Let us consider our imaging of Jesus: Do we allow the Jesus we contemplate in the Third Week's passion mysteries to affect how we understand and direct the imagining of Jesus on the cross in the first colloquy of the First Week? When we bring the fullness of our understanding to any one of the Weeks or to any elements within the Week, we will hopefully gain a greater facility in adapting the retreat and applying it to a certain individual or group.

A second prenote to our consideration of salvation may be obvious. For Ignatius, in his writing of the Exercises, there is the usual expectation that we, both director and retreatant, are coming to these Exercises with the background and culture of Christianity. Even in the ministry of some of the early Jesuits, there might be some adaptation of the Exercises for Jewish or Muslim believers. However, Catholicism or Christianity is usually the presumed context for the Ignatian retreat. Why? Because our God is a creator God, a Trinitarian God, one who creates us out of love. This God wants to share life with us forever. We also know Jesus as the Son of God, the Word in whom all things are created, the One who has redeemed us by his passion, death, and resurrection. Ignatius expects that the usual retreatant is a person who experiences the sacramental life of the church, especially the sacraments of Eucharist and reconciliation, because of his or her baptism in Christ. Acknowledging these two prenotes, let us enter into our considerations about imagining salvation.

Sin Week

The First Week of the Ignatian Exercises has often been called "sin" week. It is not unusual for those of us familiar with the Exercises to feel a certain dread at the thought of entering into the First Week. *As directors* we may be tempted to touch lightly into the First Week matter in order to spend more time with what we consider the "more important" Second Week material. *As retreatants* we hope to grit our teeth and get through some prayer period on sin and then move on in the retreat to growth or development areas in our relationship with Jesus. And yet for Ignatius the

First Week is not something just to get through or a testing to get over with. Rather, the First Week presents the essential Gospel message in Jesus' call for conversion, "repent and believe the Good News." The First Week is directed to an experience of consolation.

Ignatius and the writers of the early directories make clear that the exercises of the First Week could be given to all. In fact, according to the tradition of Ignatian retreats, the First Week exercises seem to be the ordinary retreat model. I suspect that we today would not readily feel comfortable in saying that the First Week model is the basic retreat model. Perhaps the question now is whether we can appreciate anew the true beauty and integrity of the retreat's movement that is present in the First Week considered in itself.

Through the centuries of preached retreats and parish missions, we cannot ignore the grace effect of the time-accommodated "First Week retreat"—sometimes identified as "hell week" or "sin week"—culminating in confession, the sacrament of penance. In our renewed understanding of the First Week exercises, we have stressed more the sinner's response of gratitude to a saving God or the pervading sense of being the forgiven and loved sinner. Highlighting this grace has been the source of a new appreciation of the First Week exercises even as they retain their "hardness."

But it is not just the sin material of the Ignatian First Week that presents difficulty in this Week, whether in the past or even today. We have been shaped by scriptural language and imagery and continue to be so shaped. We struggle sometimes with the picture of God it seems to paint for us, and with the kind of shame and guilt that such language seems to induce. For example, let us look at some of the references in Scripture relating to salvation/redemption. In the first letter attributed to St. Peter, we read: "You have been redeemed, not with silver or gold, but by Christ's blood beyond all price" (1 Pt 1:18-19). In the book of Revelation, we see: "For you were slain, and with your blood you purchased for God those from every tribe and tongue, people and nation" (Rv 5:9). In the Letter to the Hebrews, which builds on the Old Testament notion of sacrifice and covenant, we read: "Without the shedding of blood there is no forgiveness" (Heb 9:22); "Not even the first covenant was inaugurated without blood (Heb 9:18); "He entered, not with the blood of goats and calves, but with his own blood, and achieved eternal redemption" (Heb 9:12).

This biblical language and imagery is difficult for us Catholics in the twenty-first century to hear and understand. It may sound like a mythology of ancient times or some pagan religion; it may appear to be guilt inducing (*guilt inducing* meaning "bad" psychologically); it may be paralyzing (causing us to not know what to do).

An Ignatian Key

One key to Ignatius's understanding of the First Week is found in his setting of the colloquy of the first exercise. We have considered the place of this colloquy in both the chapter on the Faces of God and in the chapter on the Six Foundations. But it also plays an important role in our imagining salvation. Ignatius suggests a composition of place for a colloquy—the one and only time in the Exercises. He indicates not only a person that we might talk with, as he always does, but he has us also place ourselves, using the powers of our imagination, before Jesus on the cross. We remember that Ignatius proposes we approach the content material of this first prayer exercise of the Week by means of meditation, that is, through the use of our memory, understanding, and will. But in the colloquy of our prayer response in this first exercise, he calls us to use our imagination. As we gaze upon Jesus on the cross, we are encouraged to reflect on how he, who is our Creator and Lord, has come to this end, how he, who is the source of life, has given himself over to death. Then there are the Ignatian questions we ask: What have I done for Christ? What am I doing for Christ? What ought I do for Christ? We are to let whatever comes to mind be present, and so we speak out our heart to Jesus.

This last question which Ignatius poses is particularly important in the context of the First Week. As we consider, and talk with, Jesus as he is being crucified, we ask ourselves a question that looks to future action on our part, what will we be doing for Christ?

We have come to a renewed appreciation of the personalizing importance of this first colloquy, but we have not thought through carefully enough the theological meaning of this image of Jesus crucified. Yes, we are before Jesus our Savior. Yes, we do see Jesus hanging there on a cross because of love. But what do we do with all the pain and suffering, the shedding of blood—which certainly is part of our Scripture language and possibly an integral part of our lively imagination? What are our reflections on our responsibility for these afflictions, that we were being bought at a price, that Jesus' death is our ransom—again flowing from our Scripture images? Basically we all need to face the question of how we understand salvation/redemption, as it confronts us now in the image of the First Week's crucified Jesus.

The director—or, as Ignatius would say, "the one who gives"—wants to help. If our own religious understanding of the redemption is faulty, we as directors can easily let our words and approach, especially in the First Week, become an obstacle to God's grace. We as directors do not have to be theologians or, what is even more demanding, biblical scholars on the cutting edge. Nevertheless, a lot of theological work has been done in our own time that has been very important for an understanding and an articulation of the meaning of the cross, redemption, and salvation that fits more adequately the present-day mentality and is more easily understood by everyone. We might profit from reflecting a bit on our own understanding of Christian redemption for its adequacy and soundness in promoting true spiritual growth here in the First Week.

A Director's Role

We might be tempted to say that, over these past thirty years or more, the First Week has been presented as part of the Ignatian renewal quite successfully. Why would we want to bother our heads about the meaning of the First Week? Let us let God do his work. It is true that the First Week has been more often than not an effective part of the Ignatian retreat for some 450 years. Yet Ignatius would not let us easily off the hook. Ignatius was always concerned about the formation of the director. He had no doubt that God was *the* Director of the retreat. But he was also keenly aware how we human beings can become the block or barrier instead of the "help" (his favorite word to describe a minister, a director, as one who gives, as one who helps).

For Ignatius, the one who gives the retreat is the one who has had a rich experience of the Exercises. Out of that profound and holistic experience, he or she is expected to adapt the Exercises for those who are now making them and so help them to pray from their own desires. We can only adapt what we know; otherwise we will be tempted to give someone *our* experience or the experience we have read about in some book. While the Ignatian Exercises look to God's grace working with the retreatant, Ignatius at the same time places great demands upon the one who puts himself or herself forward as a director. The director must be free enough, because of his or her knowledge and not because of his or her ignorance, to sense how to adapt and apply the Exercises to the ones who are making them.

At times it is important to return to some simple but basic questions about what we ourselves know about the First Week and how we direct it. For example,

Is the emphasis on God?

What kind of God seems present in this First Week?

One who wants blood as a purchase price?

One who demands the suffering and death of his Son?

One who demands satisfaction for wrongs done?

One who likes expiation, that is, a making up for another?

One who is redeeming (buying back) from the devil (as from a co-equal?) us humans, who are being fought over like chess pawns?

Is the emphasis on us human beings?

Is the emphasis in this Week an emphasis on sin?

Is the emphasis on our feeling bad, feeling guilty?

Is the emphasis on gratitude, on thanks?

Is the emphasis on forgiving love?

Obviously these questions, and ones like them, have their psychological counterparts touching upon our sense of guilt, our sense of shame, our fear of God, our fear of hell, and our sense of wrong or sin.

How we understand or imagine redemption or salvation affects our relationship with God and with Jesus. That same understanding also affects how we view ourselves and our world. Both Scripture and our theological tradition offer us many metaphors to help us understand that God relates to us as a *saving* God. In the Old Testament and in the New, various images are used to clarify God's relationship to human beings. Words such as *sacrifice, expiation, propitiation, ransom, satisfaction, substitution* provide distinct understandings of salvation/redemption—all of them dealing with a relationship.

Sin as Mystery

Ignatius expects that, in our prayer, God will reveal sin to us, even though sin remains a mystery. Because by our ruminations we have grounded ourselves firmly on the Principle and Foundation, we acknowledge that God revealing sin to us is another of his gifts. The First Week would not make sense if it were not rooted in the Principle and Foundation consideration. In fact, Ignatius considers the Principle and Foundation so important for the dynamics of the whole retreat that he would have us continue throughout the retreat to deepen our appreciation of this Principle and Foundation by repeating it in the form of the preparatory prayer for each exercise period. And for Ignatius the key to God's revelation of sin is our conversation with Jesus on the cross—who has been identified as our Creator, the one we have known from our consideration of the Principle and Foundation. The mystery of the cross is God's response to the mystery of sin and evil as it appears in creation.

Even though the Principle and Foundation is not explicitly included with the exercises of the First Week in the Fourth and Eighteenth Annotations, the Ignatian approach to sin emphasizes that the First Week is theologically rooted in the Principle and Foundation. We know well that for Ignatius the focus in our consideration of sin is not on our particular actions or deeds, but rather on our relationship with God, which has been injured or ruptured. The injury or rupture originates with us. And so for Ignatius sin is rooted in our ingratitude and in our irreverence. Unless we have grounded ourselves firmly in the vision that God creates us for a life in relationship with him that is forever, we will be lacking in a sense of reverence. Moreover, unless we have grounded ourselves in the vision that everything is gift—that all of creation is given for us to come to know God and be able the better to respond to his love—we will not appreciate that gratitude serves as the energizing power of our life with God.

In the course of the retreat this gratitude of the First Week moves beyond a mere gratitude of words to a gratitude of deed—even to the very donation of self and the communication or sharing of what one is and has—a gratitude that marks the Ignatian prenotes about loving. As early as the Call of the King consideration, Ignatius has us retreatants listen to the prayer expressing the generous self-donation of a follower.

We might think of the Call of the King as the "mercy" meditation that completes the movement of the First Week. It is the same Jesus, to whom we have prayed as he, our Creator, is hanging on a cross; now as the Risen One, he calls us to be a part of the campaign for the kingdom of God, with victory assured. Jesus not only shares with us his saving grace, but also asks us to be with him in the work of salvation, the coming of the Kingdom. We observe the generous response of a follower in the Call of the King, but we are not asked to make this kind of response at this time. How are we to respond to Jesus now?

Jesus on the Cross

Jesus on the Cross in the colloquy of the First Week is necessarily the same Jesus we will meet in our contemplations of the passion in the Third Week. In both of those Weeks our approach to the notions of redemption, covenant, and salvation as they are imaged in Jesus has to be consistent. While Ignatius continues to ground us in the reality of the Principle and Foundation through the preparatory prayer before each exercise, he seems to nuance the foundation idea in the first prayer period of each of the succeeding Weeks, as we have examined in chapter 7. Although one can see the Call of the King consideration as a kind of "mercy" meditation closing the First Week, this same consideration has traditionally been called the "second foundation" for the Second and succeeding Weeks which deal with Gospel contemplation.

As we noted in chapter 7 on the foundations, we have not so clearly identified the Last Supper contemplation, which begins the Third Week, as serving the function of a particularizing foundational piece. When we consider its structure, it appears foundational for all the exercises that make up the Third Week. In the points of this prayer exercise, Ignatius stresses first the paschal lamb supper and Jesus' prediction of his death, then his washing of the disciples' feet, and finally his institution of "the most sacred sacrifice of the Eucharist, to be the greatest mark of his love" [289].

Let us look in greater detail at the Ignatian points for this prayer period. Ignatius gives the points for the contemplation on the Last Supper in this way [289]. First, he recalls the Passover ritual of the paschal lamb supper, in which the remembrance of the blood of the sacrificial lamb sprinkled on the door posts and lintels means deliverance from death (the angel of death *passes over*), eating the lamb meal provides strength for the journeying, and the exodus from Egypt under God's lead as a cloud by day and a fire by night eventually leads the Israelite people to a promised land and freedom. Then he stresses the simple, everyday service that embodies the work of self-donation modeled by Jesus when he washed the feet of his followers. And finally Ignatius highlights the sacrifice of the Eucharist as the greatest mark of Jesus' love. For Ignatius, it is as if our contemplation of the Last Supper, inasmuch as it is foundational, provides the key for the interpretation of all the rest of the passion mysteries. But it does require some interpretation on our part. Let us consider some of the helpful knowledge that we as directors might bring to this prayer period on the Last Supper.

Besides the Passover ritual in the Old Testament, God uses a covenant sealed in blood to relate to his people, following the secular customs of the Semitic peoples. The major exception to the sealing in blood is the rainbow covenant with Noah, often identified as a cosmic or whole-creation covenant. Blood for the Israelites signifies not death, but life; that life is the life shared between two parties. At the Last Supper, Jesus is sharing a new covenant sealed in his blood. This covenant is life giving, freeing, delivering from death, uniting with God. For Jesus, this action of sharing his life is a labor of love, humbling, without limits—as symbolized in the washing of feet. The whole of the passion is to be understood in the light of the Last Supper action. We have already alluded to the three extra points in the contemplations of the Third Week. In addition to the usual Ignatian contemplation points—seeing the people, listening to what they are saying, and watching what they do—Ignatius gives three points that stress the interior dispositions of Jesus. To be able to pray the contemplations of the Third Week, we must allow Jesus to guide us into his experience. We cannot remain observers of an event. That is why the grace of this Week is compassion—it is a *one-ing* with Christ in his passion.

Knowing such dynamics within the Third Week, how do we directors listen to how the retreatant's colloquy with Jesus on the cross is proceeding in the First Week? We remember that, when we are retreatants, we pray for the grace of "shame and confusion" in our first prayer period. Where does such a grace come from? The shame and confusion cannot simply be self-induced and still be a grace. Rather we see how Jesus tries to share with us *his* shame and confusion at our human meanness and our sin. Jesus, so totally identified with us as Son of Man, feels not anger or bitterness at our human rejection, but only shame and confusion with us in the face of our human sinful behavior. *That* may be a part of our conversation with Jesus on the cross. When we look at the big picture of evil presented in this first exercise and know the injustice of our contemporary world, we can enter into Jesus' sense of shame at our human misbehavior and meanness, at human sin—our human inhumanity to our own kind. We too are left confused. In the following prayer period, which deals with our own personal sin history, we find that the grace of sorrow and tears flows naturally as God's gift to us through Jesus.

Immediately on the first day of the First Week Jesus on the cross gives us a face of God we did not see in our consideration of the God of our Principle and Foundation. A God who waits, a God who seeks, a God who forgives more readily and more quickly than we can confess our sin—this is the face of God that Jesus on the cross allows us to see.

Salvation in the First Week

How then do we answer the questions raised earlier about the First Week? Is the emphasis on God? Yes, the emphasis in this First Week, as in every other Week of the Exercises, is on a new understanding of, and consequently a new relationship with, God. Given a sound approach to God as he is imaged in the Principle and Foundation, we are led through our prayer with the crucified Jesus to a wholly new depth of relationship with God. For this is a God who loves so much that he suffers our shame and confusion, that he sorrows and sheds tears with us, and that he forgives and saves us, and continues to share divine life with us. Our hearts, humbled and sorrowful, swell with gratitude in the face of such Love, the face of Jesus.

How then do we hear the language of God buying and ransoming, of paying a blood price, of seeking satisfaction from the bloody death of his Son? We need some familiarity with the Passover ritual and with the covenant notion of the Old Testament peoples. The Passover ritual is a commemoration of God acting to set free the Israelite people from their bondage; the ritual celebrates both the eating of the lamb and the application of its sacrificial blood to house doorways to sav those within from death. Because of the straightforward imagining of itsstory, we seem to find it easier to assimilate an understanding of the Passover event and its ritual than anunderstanding of covenant. We need to make ourselves more familiar with the notion of covenant.

In the Semitic world, a covenant between two parties was sealed by the blood of an animal. The blood represented life, not death. The blood was sprinkled on both parties—in the particular covenant of Moses, on the altar representing God and on the Israelite people—as a sign that they now shared in the same life-giving blood. When Jesus established the new covenant in his blood, he lived it out in his own death on the cross, but sacramentally he also brought all of us into this new life-giving relationship with God in the

Eucharist. Our Scripture language gropes to find images and symbols which can express the meaning of God's action in Jesus' death on the cross. The biblical notion of covenant, though still imperfect, takes on transcendent meaning in the Eucharist. In a similar way, the biblical notion of *redemption* and *redeemer* involve taking on a familial or blood relationship with the one who is being saved from debt or from wrongdoing. Other images taken more from secular society, such as ransom and satisfaction and substitution, become less and less adequate theologically.

We have an expression, "love costs." We know that, to be loving, one does "pay a price." But when we use the expression "love costs," we are not thinking that we must "purchase something" or "pay someone off." To us who love, the cost is internal. In scriptural language about the death of Jesus, we need to remember that this is the kind of cost involved—the cost of love. But certain other expressions and images become more troublesome than helpful as societies and cultures change. The importance for us as directors is to know enough not to let image or symbol language hinder the retreatant's ability to respond. At the same time, remembering Ignatius's Second Annotation, we will not set out to dazzle a retreatant with our theological or scriptural acumen, which may only get in the way. We directors will try to be helpers and wise guides.

If the emphasis is on God, in this First Week is there also an emphasis on us human beings? How could there not be? Yet the colloquy with Jesus on the cross rivets our attention on another—Jesus—right at the beginning of the First Week when the tendency may be to become fixated on ourselves. From his own experience and from his working with so many other retreatants, Ignatius has come to know that a desolation likely comes upon the person who prays the exercises of the First Week. But Ignatius seeks, not to save the person from desolation, but to direct the desolation to become spiritual, rather than to allow it to remain, or to grow even more isolating and self-fixating. His strategy is to move us through a spiritual desolation to a spiritual consolation; this is seen clearly in his direction to relate us to Jesus in his saving action. There is an emphasis in this Week on sin and our ownership of it, but the emphasis is not on our feeling bad or guilty. Rather, the emphasis is on our felt need for salvation, our need for God, a saving God. There is also an emphasis on our seeing the face of this forgiving love in the face of Jesus. The consoling grace of this Week is gratitude to a loving and forgiving God, as seen in the face of Jesus.

The First Week, then, guides us into the experience of imagining salvation. As a result of our First Week prayer, we are poised to listen to Jesus' imagining each one of us called to be working with him in bringing about this salvation. That imagining on the part of Jesus about each one of us will be seen in the Call of the King consideration, which bridges the First and Second Weeks. In this First Week, we have entered into a new understanding and a new relationship with God—our God is a saving God, a loving and forgiving God, a God choosing us forgiven sinners to be part of his family.

Chapter Ten

THE FIRST WEEK: EXPERIENCING
GOD'S JUSTICE

We seldom think of the First Week in its relation to God's justice, even though the interrelationship of faith and justice has been stressed in current church documents and practice. All of us Christians have been called to a greater social awareness as an integral part of our lived spirituality. A retreat director must be alert to the questions about justice which may arise for retreatants in the First Week.[1] For us as directors such an awareness is as essential as our being familiar with the notion of an active God or a world of gifts or a pervading response of gratitude. The director, "to be a help," must be familiar with the kinds of justice concerns that the Spirit has been inspiring in contemporary retreatants who now bring these same concerns into the retreat.

Ignatius struggles to find words expressive of his deepest experiences and God-given insights. His words seem to act more as if they point towards the meaning rather than give sharp definition. This accounts for his indifference to the discrepancies in language expressions we find between the approved Latin text and his Spanish Autograph. The experience of the Exercises "from within"—the experience of the retreatant—sheds more light on words and expressions in the written text than does any parsing analysis of Ignatius's words. His struggle as a writer is exemplified by his use of the word *sentir*. Much has been written about Ignatius's use of *sentir* to express one's relationship with the church. We remember that Ignatius brings a great love and reverence for the church, the church reality whose description he gives in this order: 1) true spouse of Christ Our Lord; 2) our holy mother the church; 3) hierarchical [353]. This kind of reverential love for a church with a human face and at the same time for a church with its authoritative

---

[1] The ideas about justice in the First Week were first presented at the annual assembly of the U.S. Jesuit Retreat and Renewal Ministries conference at Campion Center in Weston, Massachusetts, in April 2001. A version of that presentation was published in *Ignis* 30, no. 3 (2001): 3-14.

structures is the context for his *sentir* process. *Sentir* calls us to seek a meaning from within ourselves; it points us to a more holistic or comprehensive familiarity. For example, Ignatius would not be content to ask the question: What does a particular church document say? Rather he would seek to know the context, he would want a familiarity with the whole document, he would desire to develop a feel for its tone. He would want as much as possible to read the particular document "from within." That would be his *sentir* approach. Within this kind of contextual framework, let us look at Ignatius's use of the word "justice."

The Ignatian Use of "Justice"

Ignatius uses the word *justicia* or "justice" seven times in his book *Spiritual Exercises*—three times in the First Week, twice in the Contemplation to Attain Love, and twice in scriptural references dealing with the public life of Jesus in the Second Week.

In the First Week, Ignatius refers to the "original justice" enjoyed by Adam and Eve in the garden when he proposes the context of their sin in the first exercise [51]. He then suggests, in the second exercise, a reflection on the comparison between "God's justice" and "my iniquity" [59] and on the aspect of "angels as being the sword of God's justice" [60]. In the Contemplation to Attain Love, Ignatius refers twice to justice. The first time, Ignatius asks us to reflect on ourselves, "considering with much reason and justice," what we can share with a God who shares so much with us [234]. The second use of justice refers to how all good things and gifts flow from above—"justice, goodness, pity, mercy, and so on" as rays shine down from the sun, and rain waters flow from the clouds [237]. Finally, in his points for the mystery of Jesus' baptism at the Jordan by John the Baptist, Ignatius points out that Jesus, confronted by the reluctance of John, says, "Do this for the present, for so it is necessary that we fulfill all justice" [273]. When suggesting the Beatitudes as a Scripture passage, Ignatius presentsJesus saying, "Blessed . . . those who suffer hunger and thirst for justice" [278].

These citations of Ignatius's use of the word *justice* give evidence that he is always working within the biblical context. He does not seem to pay attention to social justice as such anywhere in the Four-Week structure of the Exercises. We might give some credence to a social-justice awareness on the part of Ignatius in the *reglas* or guidelines he gives under the heading "In the Ministry of Distributing Alms" [337].[2] But we cannot look to the text of the Exercises for today's awareness of social justice, social sin, sinful structures, or the communal sense of sin that goes beyond privatized sin. Some retreatants will already be well advanced in awareness of this sense of justice before entering into the retreat, others less well acquainted with such concepts.[3]

Whatever may be the retreatant's background, we can and must position our more contemporary quest for biblically rooted justice in an experience of God, such as we can find in the First Week of the Exercises.

We often identify justice with a balance sheet. Our image of justice may be formed by the common depiction of the Greek-styled woman holding scales. We hear "an eye for an eye, a tooth for a tooth," not as a statement of vengeance, but as a traditional idea of justice that we have made our own. Through his teaching and storytelling, Jesus clearly indicates that such an interpretation of justice has no convergence with the way a saving God sees life. Justice based on rights, justice based on equal balances, may approach a good philosopher's or civil libertarian's idea of justice. But it is perhaps no more than the threshold of a Christian understanding of justice. To paraphrase a Hopkins-like expression, too often "justice injustices."

Ignatius knew nothing of our contemporary struggles with the understandings of justice and our Jesuit-expressed ideal of "the service of faith of which the promotion of justice is an essential part." Yet he provides a movement in the First Week of the Exercises in which each one of us as a retreatant experiences God's justice. If we experience God's justice, will we too be rooted in God's justice? Or is there the possibility that we will be like the unjust steward of Jesus' parable, who, once forgiven his entire debt, exacts a full payment from a fellow servant whose debt is far less? That question remains ours to respond to in every age and in every circumstance,

---

[2] Consider the essay of Peter-Hans Kolvenbach, SJ, "Social Justice and the Spiritual Exercises of Ignatius Loyola" in *The Road to La Storta* (St. Louis: Institute of Jesuit Sources, 2000).

[3] Note the observation of Joseph Veale, SJ, that people who are deeply moved by injustice and feel their powerlessness are already disposed for the prayer of the First Week. See "The First Week: Practical Questions" in Philip Sheldrake, SJ, ed., *The Way of Ignatius Loyola* (St. Louis: Institute of Jesuit Sources, 1991), 59.

whether we are Peter Claver in the seventeenth century or Ignacio Ellacuría in the twentieth century or some "unjust steward" of our own twenty-first century. *That* is matter for a retreat.

Biblical Justice

In the Bible, the word *justice* used in relation to God means that God is and acts always true to Self. This notion of justice as applied to God seems to take form from the covenant idea. In the covenant, both parties had promised to live in relationship to each other in a certain way. In the biblical covenants, God takes a people to be peculiarly his own. Although at times God seems, in the biblical words of Moses, the judges, and the prophets, to threaten to destroy the relationship established by the covenant, God's consistent trait—ever emphasized by all the writers of Scripture—is faithfulness. God, being true to Self, is the faithful One, the steadfast One, the compassionate One, the forgiving One.

In his famous parable of the prodigal son, Jesus paints the classical picture of God as the Just One. We can read the entire parable and the relationships of its three characters in terms of justice. The younger son wants what is just—his inheritance—right now. The father does not dispute his claim, and promptly gives him his rightful share. When the son has squandered it all and is thus reduced, as he imagines it, to being a mere hired hand back in his father's household or perhaps even a beggar at the gates, the father rushes out to meet the returning son and quiets his confessions of wrongdoings with a total acceptance back into the family and even a welcome-home party. The elder son, however, has his own ideas of justice: You work for what you get. Neither son understands the father's sense of justice because it is a picture of divine justice that Jesus is painting. God's justice means that God remains always true to who he is—loving, compassionate, steadfast, faithful. And so God acts justly. Both sons receive God's justice—a justice of relationship that is always lovingly constant.

Experiencing God's Justice

Ignatius has his own way of drawing us into the experience of God's justice. Our consideration of the Principle and Foundation has brought home to us our basic relationship with God. God creates us with a view to sharing life with us forever; everything else is created to help us know God and better respond to him in love. Among all these created things that God has provided for us, we have choices to make and we need to make them according to how they help us to know God better and so more surely to share God's life. As we consider this foundation of our life, we naturally turn our focus to those choices of ours that have not given us life or brought us closer to God. Thus, the natural flow into the First Week material comes out of this acknowledgement of our basic relationship with God. It is analogous to the notion of "original justice" that Ignatius identifies with Adam and Eve. Their easy relationship with God is imaged in their walking in the garden with God in the twilight of the evening. This familiar relationship with God is being "true to who we are"—the "original justice" in our first parents. As Ignatius paints the picture, this is the justice they lost in their sin of disobedience, with the result, then, that they lived all their life in many labors and in much penance, outside the garden (that is, as we might interpret the phrase, outside the "home of right relationships").

Although Ignatius does not use the word *justice* in giving the first point on the sin of the angels, he does indicate that they have not used their liberty to respond in reverence and obedience to the God who has created and graced them. And so they are changed from grace to malice, from heaven to hell. For the angels and for Adam and Eve, what is evident is the change in relationship. In the beginning, angels and humans do not remain true to themselves, but try to be something—in relationship to the One who created them—that they are not created to be. For us humans, the relationship with the God who creates and gifts is disrupted, and this alienation seeps into all of our human relationships. This is why Ignatius suggests that, in the composition of ourselves for this first prayer period, we imagine ourselves feeling bound and "exiled among brute beasts" [47]. We enter into the experience of alienation even as we enter into this prayer time.

What stands out in the approach Ignatius takes to sin in this first exercise of the First Week is his focus in the colloquy with Jesus on the cross. For here we see God's response to sin. Ignatius has carefully identified Jesus as Creator and so consciously relates this colloquy to our consideration of God in the Principle and Foundation. We are being helped to understand that the history of sin runs parallel to the history of creation. Our creator God is always a saving God. Perhaps original justice applies analogously to God and to our first parents. For God is always the "original" Just One—the loving and saving God. As we have seen in the previous presentation, Jesus on the cross presents the face of *this* God, a face that represents faithfulness no matter the cost of love.

In the famous Ignatian setting of the Trinity gazing down upon the world, which is presented in the first prayer period of the Second Week, Ignatius highlights that the three divine Persons see human relations gone awry—people in blindness, dying and going to hell. It is the tragedy of this pervasive alienation—the situation of sin, whether we see it as privatized sin or social sin—that calls forth God's response in time: the response we know as Jesus, Son of God, Savior. It seems to me that we as directors bring the experience of this "bigger picture" to the first exercise on sin in creation, or sin of the world, or sin viewed objectively [50–52].

In the second prayer exercise of the First Week, we have two more uses of the word *justice*. In moving from an objective picture of sin—sin which is "out there" from the very beginning even to our own day—to a subjective overview of personal sin, Ignatius suggests we reflect on contrasts between God and ourselves. Particularly he mentions the contrast between God's justice and our own iniquity. The contrast, I believe, is between what God is—true to Self—and what we become when we act contrary to what we are or are called to be. So the expression *God's justice* means not merely that God is just or acts justly, but more correctly that God *is Justice*, in the way we are used to saying "God *is Love*." By contrast, our iniquity is not what we *are* but it is what we are doing to ourselves. Our *iniquidad*—Ignatius's Spanish word—refers to our unrighteousness resulting from the break in our relationship with God. In one of those paradoxical Scripture insights, St. Paul says that "God made him who did not know sin, to be sin" (2 Cor 5:21). Jesus becomes sin—something that no one of us humans can accomplish. We sin, but we are not sin.

In the second use of *justice* in this same second prayer period, Ignatius describes angels as being the swords of God's justice. And yet Ignatius goes on to describe these same angels—with great wonder—as enduring us, guarding us, and praying for us. The angels, just as God is true to himself, are true to themselves. Their guardianship of us through love and care and constant watchfulness is the extension of God's steadfastness. Angels are the signs of God's continuing justice stance towards us, even in the midst of our history of personal sin. The response called for in the colloquy in this second prayer period is just a cry of wonder and of thanks for experiencing a justice of God that defines him as the loving, forgiving, faithful God throughout the whole of our life.

Sharing God's Justice

As we previously observed, it is important that we as directors let our complete experience and knowledge of the Exercises influence our direction of a retreatant in any one Week or element of a Week. For example, we need to look at and acknowledge the use of *justice* in the prayer exercise called the Contemplation to Attain the Love of God that completes the Fourth Week.

In the first point Ignatius suggests that we try to make a response to God who showers gifts upon us, naming explicitly creation and redemption and then all the other particular gifts which are ours. He raises the question: What can be our response, "with reason and with justice," to God who gives so much to us? [234]. In this use of the word *justice*, we can see that Ignatius is hinting at the fact that justice, for a person of faith, is beyond reason. We are being asked to use both reason and justice in considering how we can respond to God. Aware of the biblical meaning of justice, we will respond in such a way that we remain true to who we are or are called to be, that is, sons and daughters of God.

In the second instance, Ignatius speaks of God's justice pouring forth like rays from the sun. The question for us is: Where does "our" justice come from? As Ignatius insistently points out, from the Principle and Foundation onwards through the retreat, everything is a gift from God. Justice finds its source in God. What God shares with us is the justice identifiable with God's Being. This justice that God shares with us he expects us to share with others. Here in the Contemplation we find the "completion" of the justice introduced in the First Week. God sharing his justice with us is the source of justice that flows out into our lives. Insofar as we experience and drink from the justice of God in our own life will we be enabled to work for a justice that has its origin in God. To use another image, this divine justice is the "soul" for whatever "body" or concrete form our human justice takes.

Let us consider the use of the word *justice* in the two point-citations from Scripture given by Ignatius. In the baptism of Jesus, Ignatius refers to John's reluctance to baptize and to Jesus' response, "Do this for the present, for so it is necessary that we fulfill all justice" [273]. What might this usage of *justice* mean? Does Ignatius suggest that Jesus is simply saying, This is the way it is; it is truly right and just that you, the baptizing prophet, should baptize me in acknowledgement of my relationship of obedience to God? Or is Jesus saying to John, Each one of us—you, John, and I, Jesus—is "true to ourselves" in this action, and so we fulfill all justice? Regardless of interpretation, justice is again shown to be rooted in relationship and truth.

In his Scripture citation for the Sermon on the Mount, Ignatius refers in his first point to the eight beatitudes, briefly citing them, including "those who suffer hunger and thirst for justice" [278]. Plain-sense meaning might tell us that this expression points to those people who are identified by Jesus as truly graced because they have such deep desires for the righteousness which is identified with God. Jesus says that those people are truly blessed or favored by God with whom God shares his justice—a relationship in which they experience the truth of their being "with God" which flows into their living out this truth with everyone and everything in this world. Blessed are they who embody God's justice in their everyday life. Just as we reflect spiritually that Jesus is sharing with us his way of living as he speaks out the Beatitudes, so those identified as "blessed" share the life of Jesus, the Just One.

The *number of times* that Ignatius uses the word *justice* in the whole of the Exercises is not all that significant. But *how* he makes use of the word in those different settings can lead to important reflections for us as directors and retreatants. We can truly say that the First Week is an experiencing of God's justice for ourselves. To deliberately bring the notion of justice into our direction of the First Week can provide rich insight and be a special gift for the retreatant.

Following the Just One

The importance of this kind of reflection is that it lays a foundation for our own understanding of Jesus' public life and ministry. How are we to drink in Jesus' way of responding to social inequities, to prejudice, to human degradation in all its forms? We have already acknowledged that we cannot expect to find in the ancient Scriptures how we are to identify the justice issues of our world today. We cannot search the Scriptures for any words or actions of Jesus that would give us the "answers" for what we are to say and to do. Justice, in its many secular faces, is complex; yet these are the very complexities that we must dialogue about with fellow believers and unbelievers alike. Working for justice demands the cooperation of people of faith and those of no faith.

The genius of the Exercises is that they are "exercises." The content which we bring is necessarily the Scripture, God's word, and our own life experience, including our awareness and our concern. For example, as Ignatius presents the Call of the King, he identifies Jesus as making *now* the call to every man, woman, and child. This is the post-resurrection Jesus, the Jesus who "sits at the right hand of the Father." This same Jesus makes an appeal to join the campaign to live and work for his values in the world in which we live now. The world in which we are being called to be with Christ in our labors is the real world we come up against everyday in the newspapers, on TV, and in our church and neighborhood. It demands a social awareness in all of us.

Similarly, in the meditation of the Two Standards of the Second Week, Ignatius confronts us with two value systems. It is not a meditation involving choice; we do not have to choose between the standard of Lucifer and the standard of Christ. But we as retreatants are begging for the grace to understand the values of Christ and the grace to imitate the "true life" of Jesus. What should be obvious is that our personal following of Christ and our taking on his values leads to public acts. We cannot privately imitate Christ's values of poverty, powerlessness, and humility and then find ourselves publicly acting on values associated with Lucifer. The Three Classes of Persons is meant to test the honesty of our life—are we being true to the "true life" of Jesus?

If our experience of the First Week is an experience of God's justice, we provide for ourselves a foundation on which to build a life that integrates justice into a life of faith. Retreatants, like ourselves as directors, must still discern the lead of God for their own call to incarnate their involvement. The first and most important step has already been taken: God shares justice with us, and like all lovers, we too must share this justice with others and with our world.

Chapter Eleven

THE KING: A GOD WHO BECKONS

We know that the bridging day between the First Week and Second Week of the Exercises is identified with the exercise named the Call of the King or more popularly known as the Kingdom meditation. The Call of the King has two parts: the first part is commonly identified as a parable, or story example, of a human leader making an appeal to followers, and the second part is an application of the parable to Christ and to his call. The exercise is often described as a second Foundation. With its light schedule of two prayer periods on the same matter, this exercise day seems to give the basis for the common practice of "break days" or "repose days" between the Weeks of the retreat.

A Mercy Consideration

When the Call of the King is viewed as a "mercy" consideration, it belongs more properly to the First Week. How is it seen as a mercy reflection period? When Jesus issues his call to every man, woman, and child to be with him and to join in the very enterprise dealing with the reign of God, we are made aware that the saving action of God does not leave us passive and only recipients of God's action. Jesus invites us to enter into the action with him; he invites our participation. We know the common analogy of a father building a tree house for his son and presenting it all built or a father inviting his son into the very building of the tree house. Likewise, the mother who makes and bakes the cookies herself and then offers them to her child or the mother who invites her child to help mix the cookie batter and shape them on the tray for baking.

In a similar way, Ignatius is presenting us with a God who does not leave us as passive recipients of his care, but invites us to join with him in his divine saving action. As we come to the end of the First Week, we may feel that we are only recipients of God's saving action. But the Call of the King exercise changes all this. God does not leave us mere recipients of his saving action, but invites us to be actively engaged with him in the work of salvation. This is how we understand the mercy of God, who involves us as participants in its extension. An involved participation is a special nuancing of forgiveness and mercy, giving it divine meaning. We are seeing another face of our merciful God.

A Call Consideration

When we understand the Call of the King consideration as introductory to, but integrated with, the Second Week matter, then we find the emphasis is given to the person of Christ and his life. Who is this who invites us to be with him, and to live and work with him? Because we are moved to respond to his call, we seek the grace in the Second Week contemplations: "to know Jesus more fully that we may love him more intimately so that we might follow him more closely." We are naturally led, through the Second Week prayer exercises, into the contemplations of Jesus' life and mission.

What do we learn about God in the Call of the King consideration? We see, first of all, that the initiative comes from Christ. Christ does the calling *now*, just as he has done the calling in the Gospel passages. That is the Ignatian perspective. We observe that, theologically, we might say more correctly that the initiative is from God the Father. We see the expression of this initiative when, in the Gospel Transfiguration passage, God's voice thunders out: This is my beloved Son. Listen to him. Regardless of how we attribute the initiative back to the Trinitarian relations, the initiative is always from God (as in God's first call to us in creating us). We remain respondents to one more gift of God in Jesus—the call.

The common word we use—*call*—does not capture well the quality of the initiative taken by God or by Christ. Jesus does not issue an invitation or call in which he has no personal feeling or involvement. I believe that, because Jesus is on fire with his mission, we can rightly say that "Jesus beckons." He puts his whole self into the call; his voice is strong, his eyes invite, his arm and hand reaches out and draws us in. There is a charge, like an electrical charge, proper to the way Jesus invites his followers, so the felt seriousness of his call is better caught in our word *beckons*. Jesus wants us to be with him; he wants us to labor with him. His "wanting" is what we are trying to capture in the word *beckons*. What *beckons* does not include is any sense of duress. When God beckons, despite all his loving desire, he waits. God will keep calling because he is the faithful one. But God waits on our response. Our human response to God must always be willing and free.

At the same time that the Call of the King is an exercise focused on this beckoning, it is also an exercise about dreams. Ignatius couches it in terms of a story of a human king calling for a crusade. It reflects the dream that first fired Ignatius, but it is a dream that is persistent in the epics and stories in many of our human cultures. The content of the call is the stuff of which our human dreams are made.

Jesus' Dream

As Ignatius presents it, this myth story is meant to help us understand the Gospel preaching of Jesus. Jesus has a dream; it is God's dream. Jesus calls every man and woman and child to enter into that dream with him. When in our prayer we bring our life dreams into the dream of Jesus, we find how we are to use all the talents and drives and passions that are God's gifts to us. We allow God to transform our drives and passions in ways that we could never have dreamed of.

Ignatius clearly presents to us the double aspect of the call of Christ. Jesus calls each one of us into a special relationship with him and, in and through that special relationship, to work with him for the reign of God by "being busy about the Kingdom." In the Call of the King exercise, Ignatius has us reflect on our dreams, our goals, our life desires. We need to look at our dreams in these terms: Who is Jesus for us? What place does Christ have in our life? What is our relationship with Jesus, and how does it affect our way of thinking and dreaming about life? Have we considered seriously Jesus' dream about the reign of God and his invitation to us to be together with him and labor with him? Ignatius lets us hear, in the response of the generous ones, how they want and desire to have their dreams shaped by the dream of Jesus. We are never meant to give up our dreams, but we are called to let God help shape them.

A Prayer Time

We have identified this prayer period of the Call of the King as a *consideration* when we were naming the Ignatian ways of praying in chapter 5. Distinct from the Principle and Foundation consideration, it does have a prelude of asking for a grace. We ask for the grace not to be deaf to Christ's call, but to be ready and diligent to respond. But the Ignatian structure keeps the matter objective, and, in place of our speaking out our own response (a colloquy), we listen to the prayer response of those who want to be more devoted and to signalize themselves in their service to their Lord. Ignatius does not ask us to join our voices with theirs in this colloquy; rather he asks only that we listen to them and drink in their example. In its own way, the Call of the King consideration is meant to be a preliminary signal for us retreatants about the readiness that we see in the Third Type of Person (or the Third Class of Men). We desire to hear Christ's call to us, and we want to be able to enter our dreams and allow them to be shaped into his dreams. In our ruminating on this matter two times during the day, we may find ourselves telling God of our desire to be identified with the great-hearted people or, at least, the desire for that desire. This consideration truly provides the bridge into the Second Week.

Jesus shows us, then, the face of a God who beckons. We relate to a God who wants us to be with him, who wants to share with us and involve us in the work of salvation. In the Ignatian dynamics, both God and we ourselves connect with a new energy, not experienced in the Principle and Foundation exercise. We come to know a God who calls us to enter into his dreams and then waits for us, with all our own dreams, to respond. And so we enter expectantly into the Second Week contemplations.

Chapter Twelve

VALUES RELATED TO VISIONS
AND STRATEGIES

Understood as a dynamic movement, the Ignatian Exercises flow with an interplay among three basic components: visions, values, and strategies. Some individual exercises stand out clearly as focusing on vision or value, but many exercises seem to cross over and blend, giving equal emphasis to vision and value, or value and strategy, or any combination of the three.

An Overview

Three exercises clearly stand out as providing us primarily with a vision. The Principle and Foundation, the Call of the King, and the Contemplation on the Love of God set forth refinements of the basic Christian vision of God and us and the world. All three of these exercises focus on our clarifying what it is we see and how we see it, in terms of God's relation to us. At the same time that they present a vision or a dream or a certain life ideal, they necessarily include suggestions of the values that are integral to such an ideal or dream. The Two Standards and the Three Types of Persons are summary exercises dealing with values. There follow, then, some ways to make the vision our own, realize our dreams, and work at the values integral to the vision. These methods of working at or accomplishing those values are the strategies that Ignatius presents throughout the Exercises. The various examens, the many ways of praying, environmental helps like light and darkness, the use or nonuse of penance, the retreat conferences themselves are all part of the strategies that Ignatius proposes to help us in the good movement of the retreat.

A Value Day

One day uniquely stands out in the Exercises for its presentation of values, with its inherent strategies. That day is the fourth day of the Second Week. It is a day given over to a meditation-style prayer like no other day in the retreat. We are praying to understand values, especially the values of

Christ. By the Ignatian structural meditations of the Two Standards and the Three Classes, we are being readied to enter into the contemplations of Christ in his ministry and the values he presents in the Gospel mysteries.

Ignatius writes with detail when he sets up the scene for the Two Standards exercise. From the title of the exercise, we expect the Ignatian picture of a battleground—a *spiritual* battleground, but a true battleground. Although there is evidence enough of Ignatius's medieval-chivalry ideas and even crusader outlook, he seems in this exercise to rely more on scriptural imagery, especially St. Paul's various allusions to our being involved in "spiritual warfare." Ignatius has us picture two camps, each flying its flag or standard.

In the one camp, we see Lucifer (Ignatius carefully chooses this name over other possibilities such as Satan or Beelzebub). The very name *Lucifer* means "bearer of light," and there will be a reference to the evil angel "who takes on the guise of an angel of light" [332] in the Ignatian *reglas* or guidelines for discernment (discussed in chapter 16). Lucifer is pictured seated on a great chair (throne), but obscurely seen because of the fire and smoke. The setting is Babylon—a place name in *this* world and a name from the Hebrew Scriptures (Gn 11:9) now connoting noise, din, and a great mixture of languages breaking down all communication. Babylon has also come to symbolize exile. Lucifer can be heard to be commanding and scattering his minions (demons) to enslave and bind with chains everyone everywhere, ensnaring them in nets, tempting them to long for riches (usually the first temptation in most cases, Ignatius adds), to thereby come to accept vain honor from the world, and to then be consumed with vast pride. Lucifer indicates that, if these cravings trap people, they will then be led to all manner of other vices.

In the other camp, we see Jesus as he is pictured in St. Luke's Gospel at the time of the Sermon, commonly identified as the Sermon on the Mount because of its setting in St. Matthew's Gospel. For Luke, though, Jesus is "on the plain"—on the same level as all of us who are watching and listening. Jesus is in the field of Jerusalem, a city whose name means "peace of God," not a place of exile, but a symbol of home. When we listen to Jesus, he is not ordering or commanding or scattering. He invites, he chooses, and he sends his disciples and followers throughout the world. Jesus' intention is *to help* all people by bringing them to the highest spiritual poverty and, if God so chooses, to actual poverty. Such people will then experience a kind of contempt from others who hold different values. But these people, followers of Christ, will come to know true humility. Living in this way, these people will shine out in all manner of other virtues.

A Questioning of Values

We have often piously presented this prayer exercise as if Lucifer's values were blatantly bad and Jesus' values were obviously good. But I do not believe that this is the picture Ignatius is painting for us. When he has us pray for the grace of *understanding*, Ignatius is indicating his presumption that we do not naturally make sense out of Jesus' values. In fact, common sense and good psychology would suggest that our desires for Lucifer's values of wealth, respect, and a certain self-pride are healthy. We want to be successful in providing for our self and our family and in contributing to our church and society. We like to be well thought of and we have a right to our good reputation. Low self-esteem is a terrible psychological affliction, and much is made of educating children with proper self-pride. Granted that excessive self-focus on any one of these aspects of our life—having resources, being respected, or possessing a good self-image—can lead to bad consequences, still we can easily hear and understand the proper values of riches, honors, and self-pride.

If Ignatius had picked out love as the value that Jesus preached, we could easily be impressed and find it desirable. The same might be said for kindness, hospitality, or maybe, hard as it is, forgiveness. But when Jesus proposes *poverty*, spiritual surely and even material if God so gifts, and then *humiliations*—what we might today sum up in the word *powerlessness*—resulting finally in *humility*, we are inclined to consider this array just named as the signs of a failed life. In themselves, poverty, humiliations, and humility do not seem life giving and would hardly measure up on any scale of human values. So how, we ask ourselves, could Jesus ever think to rally us around this kind of a call?

Jesus' Temptations

This prayer exercise begins to lead us into the subtleties of Ignatian discernment. For we can see how the angel of light presents what is truly good—we remember from the Principle and Foundation that riches, honor, and pride are gifts from God, in no way bad in themselves—and so we are attracted. But the very attraction to these gifts draws us away from the Giver and focuses us on our own self-sufficiency. The analogy to the Matthean description of Jesus' temptations is easy enough to draw upon. Each of the temptations is in the form of a good which facilitates the accomplishment of Jesus' mission. If he could feed not just himself but a whole world (a problem still with us today), surely all would recognize and accept him as the One sent from God, the Messiah. Or if he could just take over by sheer power all the kingdoms of the world, then he would be acknowledged by all as God's chosen One, the Messiah. Or if he would do just one grandstanding act, like throw himself down from the pinnacle of the Jerusalem temple so that people could see the angels of God lift him on high, then he would be acknowledged as truly the Son of God and Messiah. Jesus' temptations can be described in terms of riches and power and pride. The temptations seem to be good inasmuch they accomplish the purpose of his life—to be accepted as Messiah. Yet, is Jesus determining the kind of Messiah he wants to be, or does he continue to seek God's lead? As Ignatius indicates in his own text, if people can be ensnared in the nets of riches, honor, and pride, then the slide into any vice is made easy. People get trapped into wanting to act like God or even into acting like God—the temptation of our first parents, the temptation of the fallen angels, the temptation of Jesus, and the continuing temptation of humankind.

Understanding by Comparison

Ignatius presumes that only insofar as we understand the values presented by Lucifer will we receive the grace of understanding Jesus' choice of values. Jesus deliberately chooses what is counter to Lucifer's chosen values, for it is their counteractivity that gives them value. Poverty in itself is not a value. Can we ever describe God as poor? How would poverty, then, make us like God? But God in Jesus did choose poverty as is affirmed in the words of the famous hymn in Philippians: "Though he was in the form of God, he did not deem equality with God something to be grasped at. Rather, he emptied himself and took the form of a slave, being born in the likeness of man" (Phil 2:6-7).

Jesus knew the poverty of total emptiness—going from being identified with the fullness of divinity to being born as a human being—described theologically as such total emptiness that even God's divinity can be accommodated. John's Gospel in particular emphasizes Jesus' words that he has nothing but what the Father gives him, not even his message being his own. He lives in an occupied country, he has no recognized academic credentials, and he has learned at best only a carpenter's trade. In the Gospels, he is put down as one coming from Nazareth, and he probably had the uncultured accent of that northern section of the country. Jesus knew not only the poverty of being human; he knew also the powerlessness of a person of little account. But these gifts of poverty and powerlessness help form for Jesus the basis of his humility.

Humility—derived from the Latin *humus* meaning "ground"—refers to a person's ground-level attitude. Humility deals with one's attitude toward the truth, the reality of what is. A humble person knows the truth of his or her being. Jesus says, "Learn from me, for I am gentle and humble of heart" (Mt 11:29). Jesus knew himself, above all, as the "beloved Son," an identity confirmed in the scriptural accounts of his baptism and transfiguration. His knowledge of his own identity—his humility—was Jesus' greatest gift from the Father—a gift that no human being has had given to him and that no one could ever take from him. Jesus shows us in himself the values of poverty, powerlessness, and humility. In Jesus we see how we can, from resting in the truth of our very being, grow in the virtuous life. Jesus presents us with a faith understanding of poverty, powerlessness, and humility. We are helped in our graced faith understanding by picturing the two opposing camps, by seeing Jesus calling us to the *hidden* values he has chosen and Lucifer countering with the *apparent* values he proposes to us as entrapments.

Ignatius always describes Lucifer, or the devil, as "the enemy of human nature." The devil is not defined as the enemy of God, but as the enemy of humankind. Lucifer is the enemy of "human nature," not so much of what it is in itself, but of what any one man or woman can become—by God's grace. We truly grow and mature as children of God. For a creature—one *created* just as Lucifer is—to become identified as a part of God's family is too much for the devil. Our being sons and daughters of God, human though we are, elicits the devil's enmity. That is why, in the Ignatian context, Lucifer has earned the title of "the enemy of human nature."

A Pair of Glasses

The fourth day of the Second Week demands hardheaded thinking because we truly struggle to understand what Christ proposes as values. In this exercise, Ignatius is, as it were, giving us glasses so that, as we read and pray the Gospels, we see Jesus' calls and invitations in a wholly new way. If we can fit ourselves with these new glasses, the paradoxes of Jesus' speech are viewed differently and they take on fresh meaning for us. The glasses, which the Two Standards exercise provides, become indispensable for our contemplations of the public life of Jesus. For it is by our seeing (as well as by hearing and observing, as in any Ignatian contemplation) that we are able to enter a new Gospel world that leaves behind the ruts of our old familiarity with passages and our usual, set patterns of understanding their meaning.

A Case Study

Ignatius learned from his own experience and from the experience of working with others in giving the Exercises that, beyond understanding, another step is necessary. After working with a retreatant through two meditation periods and then two repetitions on the matter of the Two Standards—always seeking a depth of understanding as a personal grace—Ignatius proposes a fifth and final meditation period. This prayer exercise has traditionally been called the Three Classes, and it seems to be modeled on the case-study format with which today we have an easy familiarity (for example, in the study of law or business). Ignatius likely would have learned this approach during his university time in Paris where, as a student for the priesthood, he studied moral theology, which at the time followed a case-study system called *casus conscientiae* (Latin for "case(s) of conscience").

The case-study model seems appropriate here because Ignatius's title for this exercise would literally be about three pairings (Spanish, *tres binarios*), a traditional pedagogical device of using two people, usually a man and a woman called Titius and Bertha, as representatives involved in typical human situations that present moral questions. Ignatius wants us to consider how people value decision making in life situations. Ignatius presents the setting as one in which all three pairs have acquired a large amount of money "not solely, or as they ought, for the love of God." For their own peace with God, they would like to rid themselves of the hindrance that this attachment costs them. After setting forth the situation, Ignatius describes each pair's way of deciding how to handle this affair.

Those in the first group exhibit good intentions. They acknowledge the problem of their attachment, they talk about doing something to solve it, but they keep putting off the decision. They reach the end of life and they have made no decision. The second pair also acknowledge the attachment and, instead of freeing themselves, they keep the money and at the same time work at getting closer to God. Their lack of decision about their attachment shows their expectation that God will come to them even though the block in the relationship originates with them. The third pair wants to be quit of their attachment and stands ready to keep or be rid of the money, however God may draw their desires and whatever will be made apparent to them to be better for serving God. Their decision is not to want the money or any other thing unless only the service of God moves them.

A Pair of Jogging Shoes

As we think about how these different groupings of people handle a difficult situation, we are praying for the grace to choose what is more to the glory of God and our own salvation. Ignatius lets us see that our life with God involves more than just an understanding of following; our life with God demands that we make choices and that we choose to rid ourselves of any attachments which would hinder our following of Christ and our service of God. In this prayer exercise Ignatius has—to use a different analogy—provided us with running shoes so that we can quickly move off the starter's block when we run the Pauline race to gain the crown of life. With the glasses provided by the Two Standards and the running shoes provided by the Three Classes, we have the basic equipment from this fourth day to launch into the contemplations about our following Jesus in his public ministry. As candidates for ministry profess in their ordination ceremony, so we can now say: We are "ready and willing" to listen to and follow Jesus in whatever way he invites us.

Agere Contra

Ignatius adds one more directional note to this exercise on the Three Classes. When we consider the possibility that we are not indifferent to riches or poverty, but in fact feel a repugnance to poverty, we are to ask God that he choose us for the gift of actual poverty. Ignatius encourages us to go so far as to ask and beg and entreat God so to do if it would be for the greater glory and praise of God. To pray in this way in the face of our repugnance came to be known as the Ignatian *agere contra*, meaning "to act against" or "to act in a contrary way." Ignatius knows that, although we cannot directly change our feelings, we can pray that God will more directly intervene by facilitating our freedom to choose. This final note [157] is a strategy device that Ignatius found helpful in his own experience and in his working with others. Our very praying to God for help to change is our first step in breaking whatever binds us or hinders us from movement.

Although we will continue to drink in Jesus' values through the contemplation of Gospel mysteries carefully selected by Ignatius, this fourth day plays a unique role in helping us to see and to accept the sometimes paradoxical values involved in the following of Jesus. At the end of the fourth day, we stand ready (by God's grace) to walk with the Lord in his public life—with an ability to listen to his words with greater openness and understanding, to watch his actions with sharpened vision, to observe his choices with refined sensitivity, to rise to his challenges with fear allayed, and to be open to following wherever Jesus leads.

Chapter Thirteen

THE TWINS: COMPASSION AND CONSOLATION

The Third Week and the Fourth Week are so closely related that Ignatius does not put a time interval between them. For Ignatius, there is no first day of the Fourth Week; only a first exercise is identified. In the Ignatian dynamics, the Weeks are joined by two complementary movements. In the Third Week, we seek the grace of compassion, allowing Jesus to bring us into his experience of his own passion and death. In the Fourth Week, we ask for the grace to enter into the joy and consolation of the risen Jesus. At first it may appear that the Third and Fourth Weeks have little connection with each other beyond the obvious chronology. But only if we have let the movement of the Third Week penetrate our being will we be able to understand and drink in for ourselves the movement of the Fourth Week.

The Third Week

We set forth into the Third Week, where the content material is the Gospel events of Holy Thursday, Good Friday, and Holy Saturday. The prayer form, following upon the Second Week, remains contemplation, with an Ignatian addition of three extra points for each prayer exercise, so that we let Jesus lead us into his experiences of the passion. The most important grace that we seek in our identifying with Jesus at this central moment of his earthly life is the grace of compassion.

That Jesus has died, with a lot of suffering, is history. The event has already happened and we cannot change the fact. That we can be present to Jesus in his sharing with us his passion and death is also a fact, and our desired response—the grace we pray for—is called *compassion*, a very precious gift of God to us. The temptation when we cannot do anything to change a situation is to walk away, to try to harden ourselves, to maintain an emotional distance, or to despair. In the face of these natural, understandable human responses, we all the more appreciate compassion as a difficult but priceless grace.

Compassion is first of all experienced when we stay with Jesus throughout the events of his passion. Ignatius is careful to point out that we will have to "work at" being present and involved in each of these prayer periods. Perhaps our familiarity with the passion story or maybe the expectation that prayer on these events will come easy for us make the Ignatian direction all the more necessary. We may know the experience of staying with someone dear in the last hours of life; we may have been asked to be with a spouse or a family at the time of a death. What is important lies not in what we say; the key is our loving presence. This is the stance of compassion.

By adding three points to the usual points of this prayer exercise, Ignatius emphasizes the importance of our moving "inside" the mysteries of the passion. Jesus is the one—the only one—who can give us entrance into his experience of the passion events. Ignatian contemplation is how we find Jesus inviting us into the most important work of his life, our redemption. It is as if Jesus were saying, Let me tell you what it was like, what I saw, what I felt. Please don't interrupt; just stay with me and listen. As we enter into the sights and feelings of Jesus, we find our way into compassion. Each prayer period builds upon the previous one, so that compassion is not just our feeling wounded. Compassion identifies the wound that is *us*, as we stay with Jesus in his suffering and death.

For Ignatius, compassion in all our relationships with others and in all our ministries of whatever kind is grounded in our having experienced this intimacy with Jesus, especially in his passion and death. Following Jesus and ministering with Jesus are wonderful graces flowing from the Second Week of the Exercises. But such companioning is not enough for the true disciple of Jesus. Unless the presence and activity of the disciple are stamped with the grace of compassion, we can hear the Gospel words of Jesus: "I never knew you."

The Third Week comes to a close when we are quiet and at peace while standing compassionately at the tomb of the dead Jesus. We have experienced his dying, and we have accompanied his body to the tomb. With Jesus' death, there is an emptiness, a void, a darkness, a sense of meaninglessness. Compassion enables us to stay in the loneliness.

The Fourth Week

The Fourth Week deals with our relationship with Jesus as he is right now. He is the One who is risen, who dies no more, who pleads for us at the right hand of the Father. Ignatius proposes that we pray for the grace to be able to participate in the joy and consolation of Jesus as he savors the victory of his risen life. Our readiness to enter into the joy of Jesus comes from building on the grace of the Third Week. Letting Jesus bring us into his joy, experiencing his consoling presence is like turning a coin to its other face, the first face representing our letting Jesus lead us into his passion, our experiencing compassion.

We use our insight into, and experience of, the Third Week in order to enter into and experience the Fourth Week. Our graced ability to experience the pain and grief of Jesus through our compassion, without being able to change anything of his history, allows us to appreciate how Jesus is present with us, consoling and strengthening, yet without changing the history that is ours. But the consoling presence of Jesus who promises a sure victory for us too is the joy of the Fourth Week that perdures into life after the Exercises.

Jesus the Consoler

Ignatius's favorite word to describe the risen Jesus' ministry is *consolar* ("to console"). Jesus in his risen life is, above all, a Consoler—One who strengthens, encourages, comforts, and lightens with joy. In his risen body, Jesus represents the continuity of our human life while at the same time he shows its transfigured face. Resurrection is not a resuscitated human life, such as we see after the raising of Lazarus by Jesus in John's Gospel. Resurrection is our human life transformed. At a wholly new level, our human life is now identified with "living with God" forever. This is Jesus' experience.

Following a pious tradition, Ignatius guides us into this new relationship with the risen Jesus through his appearance to Mary, his mother. As we noted in chapter 6 on the Faces of God, Ignatius makes this prayer exercise the key to our appreciating the undreamed-of depth of intimacy that the risen Jesus wants to share. Mary, with whom Jesus has known the most precious of intimacies of mother and son, is the first to experience the wholly new depth of closeness, love, and consolation that Jesus' risen presence means. If through our contemplation we become privy to this most precious moment between mother and Son, we will be enabled to grasp the import of all the other resurrection mysteries in the Scriptures.

Jesus knows that we live in a world that looks so much the same. It appears to be unchanged by the definitive victory of his resurrection. For example, the sun still rises and sets, rains and droughts still happen, plagues and floods take place, people get born and die, wars are still fought. How do we *experience* the newness of resurrection?

Our ticket or our way in—an Ignatian strategy to grow in our knowledge and experience of the Jesus we relate to *now*, the risen Jesus—is through our contemplations of the Fourth Week. Entering into our prayer, we attempt to know how it is that this risen Jesus touches us and becomes our consoler. From the New Testament passages, we drink in the consistent pattern of Jesus' consoling role: to take away fear, to give peace, and to send forth with Good News. What Jesus does in every appearance symbolizes what we as Christians committed to his mission are also to do. Whatever our lifestyle and ministry, we in some way participate in Jesus' role of consoling, taking away fear, giving peace, and sharing the Gospel. Like the first Christians, we are experiencing how Jesus "fills" our world.

Spiritual Consolation

To enter more fully into Jesus' mission, we need to understand *consolation* as Ignatius associates it with the risen Lord. Ignatius more fully describes consolation in the context of his *reglas,* guides or guidelines, for discernment (discussed with the other *reglas* in chapter 16). Among the discernment guides that are more applicable to the First Week is spiritual consolation, described by Ignatius in the third guide/guideline [316]. We note that the consolation which Ignatius wants to identify as a help in our Christian living is called *spiritual.* What makes consolation spiritual? As Ignatius indicates, consolation is spiritual insofar as it relates us to God— which is a gifting of the Spirit. We experience times of natural consolation, times of a sense of well-being. These experiences need not be what we call spiritual or graced. We also experience the afterglow period that follows upon the grace of spiritual consolation, and this kind of period too needs to be distinguished from spiritual consolation itself.

Spiritual consolation has its root in an experience of God relating us to himself. For example, Ignatius would say that we might describe three instances of consolation as follows: (1) an interior movement within us that inflames us with love of God; (2) the shedding of tears that moves to love of God; and (3) every increase of faith, hope, and charity, and every experience of interior joy that calls and attracts us to the things of God. Each time that Ignatius touches into the experience of consolation that is spiritual, he points out how the moment is always an experience that centers on God drawing us into a relationship with him. Ignatius knows from his own experience that we have times of spiritual consolation and times of spiritual desolation and also times in between, which he would identify as "times of tranquility."

Do we more commonly live in consolation, in desolation, or in the in-between? There seems to be no set answer for us human beings. But we know that God is always working with us. The question that arises for us is: Should we pray for spiritual consolation, or is it selfish or somehow "wrong" to pray for such consolation? When we consider our experience in the exercises of this Fourth Week, we understand that it is what the risen Christ wants to do for us as he did for his first followers. Jesus' abiding gift of the Spirit is meant to be a gift of consolation, bestowing strength, light, and comfort.

It is true that we are an Easter people, a people in the care and comfort of the risen Lord. Our lives, our words, our actions in ministry are all the more effective the more we remain in touch with God's consoling power. This is an Ignatian understanding of the importance of consolation in our daily lives and activity.

What we learn and experience in the Third and in the Fourth Weeks is that there are new levels of intimacy that grace our life, beyond the intimacy we prayed for in the Second Week. Compassion names this new and deeper relationship with Christ in the Third Week. Consolation—Jesus' intimate action within us—identifies us with Mary insofar as we experience a relationship so embracing that it has no limits or boundaries. We have come to know that, in our following of Christ, our evangelizing activity is not enough.

The Christian disciple is a person distinguished for acting with compassion and for sharing consolation. We find ourselves in our compassion and in our consolation being twinned with Christ.

Chapter Fourteen

LOVE COMMUNICATES

The Contemplation on the Love of God is the final prayer exercise of the Ignatian retreat. Although as a prayer exercise it is glowingly referred to in commentaries on the *Spiritual Exercises* book, I think that we seldom reflect with any depth on the dynamics that are involved in a full understanding of this particular exercise. The English translations of this exercise's title (*Contemplación para Alcanzar Amor*) usually do not identify clearly the Ignatian movement. The exercise's title is sometimes translated "Contemplation to Attain the Love of God" or "Contemplation to Obtain the Love of God." A clearer translation, not literal or succinct, but more accurately detailing the dynamics of this exercise would be: "Contemplation on the Ways That God Loves So That We Might Be Graced to Love Similarly."

The Ignatian Prenote

Ignatius presents a prenote of two points before he guides us into the text of the exercise. Both points of the prenote are essential to our understanding of *"love"* (*amor*) as Ignatius wants to use the term. The prenote's first point observes that love ought to be expressed more in deeds than in words. Then the second point emphasizes that the one who loves "communicates" (the Ignatian word *comunicar*) with the one who is loved. This communication takes shape by way of sharing whatever goods the lover has—family, friends, wealth, learning, virtue, and so on—with the beloved. And so too the beloved shares similarly with the one who loves.

There is a certain paradox in Ignatius's choice of the Spanish word *comunicar* in the second point of the prenote since in the first point he has just stressed deed over word. Yet Ignatius remains true to the basic insight he has presented in the Principle and Foundation, namely, that God is always communicating with us. In all of his gifts God is speaking to us; through the events of our life God can be heard if we listen. The prenotes that Ignatius presents come not so much from common sense or psychological insight as from his reflection on his own mystical experience of God's ways of loving, as it is evidenced by the time at Manresa he describes in his *Autobiography* [28, 29, 30]. He will so direct our prayer in this exercise that we might make his reflection our own.

The Setting

As usual, Ignatius has constructed the prayer period in a tightly integrated way. The first prelude [232] presents the picture of our standing before God in the heavenly setting, with all the angels and saints praying for us. In our contemplation, if we look around carefully, we realize that all these angels and saints are *loving* us in their very act of praying and interceding for us. The communion of saints manifests its reality in the sharing—the communicating—that is true of all lovers. The very "composing of ourselves" in this prayer exercise immerses us in the experience of loving. The second prelude expresses the grace we seek, which gives a direction to our prayer exercise. We are desiring to so recognize all the love gifts from God that we become "empowered" or "enabled" to love and serve God in every aspect of our life. We want an awareness and an appreciation of how God embraces us and rings us round with so many ways of loving that we ourselves are enabled to pour forth our love energies in our response to God in all our life situations. Simply said, we desire the grace to be able to love more and more the way that God loves.

The Four Points

Ignatius's pointing of the prayer in four ways is meant to help our relating to God through our reviewing and re-experiencing his various communications of love. If we were merely to read through the four points suggested for the prayer period, we might be inclined to think that this exercise appears to be more of a meditation style of prayer. Yet Ignatius had carefully identified it as a contemplation. Traditionally there have been various ways of explaining how this exercise truly involves us in a contemplative style of praying. The most cogent explanation of how these four points flow into a contemplative style of prayer has been expressed in recent times by Michael Buckley, SJ.[1] Let me elaborate in my own way on the contemplative understanding of the makeup of this exercise.

---

[1] Michael J. Buckley, SJ, "The Contemplation to Attain Love," *The Way Supplement,* no. 24 (1975), 92-104.

Each of the four points of the Contemplation is like a review of one of
the Weeks. As a result, there is no new matter to be chewed and digested.
Rather, each point given is meant to stimulate the memories we have of our
experiences in each of the Weeks. Certain words, phrases, or ideas in each
point give a hint of this kind of memory stimulus. The first point speaks of
gifts of God to us in creation and redemption and all the gifts special to
ourselves, such as family, friends, health, talents, and vocation. The second
point refers, not only to how God gives gifts, but also to how God shares his
very life and being with us by his presence and dwelling with us. This point
looks especially to God becoming incarnate in Jesus, who "pitches his tent"
with us. The third point recalls how God labors for us in all his gifting. But,
of course, as we know from the Third Week, the greatest labor is Jesus'
passion and death. Finally, the fourth point emphasizes how there are no
limits or boundaries to the way that God pours Self out in his love. The
image of the sun shining or a spring pouring out its waters can only help
recall the risen Jesus who has broken through all limits and boundaries in
loving us.

At the same time that we are drinking in the limitless ways of God's
loving, we find ourselves being educated and moved to express our love in
similar, though limited, ways. We, too, discover our communication with
God enlivened and deepened when we try to respond with our "giving of
gifts" that demonstrate our love, with our loving presence, with our
struggling efforts to remain true to love, and finally with our moments of
loving largesse. To try to "spell out" these interactions of love probably does
not capture what our actual prayer time was about. Our rich experience of
colloquy defies description. With that acknowledgment, let us examine more
closely the Ignatian prayer suggested as our colloquy.

The Repeated Colloquy

For the first time Ignatius does not wait till the end of the four points to
recall that a colloquy flows through our prayer, especially at its close.
Instead, he indicates, at the end of each point, that we should be making
some response to a God who so loves us as we have been reviewing in the
point's content. He gently proposes a prayer whose content gives us one
formulation of how we might respond. This Ignatian prayer, called the
Suscipe ("Take and Receive"), has been carefully structured by Ignatius and
expresses the fruit of the retreat.

If lovers communicate in their sharing, what do we have to share and what are we communicating by sharing it? If, like Jesus, we realize that we are truly poor and everything we have is gift, what can we share that we can say is in any way "ours" to share? We also need to remind ourselves that lovers share. Lovers do not take, leaving the other bereft. And so we are not giving up or giving away anything when we make this prayer. We are speaking of sharing with God just as God shares with us.

What Ignatius suggests that we offer to share first is our liberty. Since we know from one of the early Annotations [5] that the Exercises expect a retreatant to have magnanimity (Spanish, *con grande animo*) and generosity (Spanish, *liberalidad*), we are not surprised that such a person is described as offering to God all his or her liberty (Spanish, *libertad*). Without involving a particular philosophical or theological school, Ignatius seems to point to a capacity or interior talent—namely, liberty—which when exercised leads to the generosity or liberality of the great-souled person. In the very exercising of this ability to be generous, we are communicating with God about our desire to be one with him in his will. Although liberty is a gift of God, our "communicating" is the very action whereby the potential which is ours (*libertad*) is actualized in our sharing (*liberalidad*). Logically, there is no other beginning to our sharing or our communicating than to offer our liberty—a gift not actualized until it has been shared. And in so sharing, we make real our disponability or availabilty to God.

What next might we describe as belonging to us that we could share with God? Our memories are truly *our* memories, and what we remember and the way we remember is unique to us. We would like to share our memory with God. We would also like to share *our* understanding. As with our memories, what we understand and the way we understand is unique to us. We would like to share our understanding with God. Finally, what we want and what we desire—summed up in the word *will*—is what we offer to God because it is *our* wants and desires. What is our stance before God? We want, in sum, to share with God whatever we have and call our own.

As in any love relationship, we want to say what we share belongs to the one we love as much as it belongs to us. But with God as the Lover and ourselves as the beloved, we confess that everything we have, God has given and so we entrust everything to God in return. From the depths of our heart, we cry out that God's love and grace are enough for us.

The prayer is the prayer of a lover. Who can tell one who loves how to express his or her love? For this reason, Ignatius is gentle in suggesting his own prayer as the response that each one of us should make. But Ignatius's prayer is not just an effusion of love sentiments, but also a carefully structured expression of love, according to his prenote on love.

Although for lovers all words prove inadequate, perhaps when we fix on the word *freedom* as a goal of the Exercises, we do not correctly identify the dynamics made evident particularly in this exercise. We do better to point to the *generosity* or *liberality* of the great-souled person who has been thus shaped by the grace of the Exercises. But, then, there is one more stage beyond generosity—what generosity allows—our *disponability* or our *availability* before God. We truly mean "take and *receive*." After all, love always communicates. Communication—we understand now at a wholly different level—is part of the dynamics essential to the Exercises.

PART III

GIVING DIRECTIONS

Chapter Fifteen

DISCERNMENT: HEART AND HEAD

Ignatius's writings on discernment have probably earned him his greatest fame among the spiritual traditions of Catholicism and in the wider world of spiritualities. For Ignatius, discernment is not just a retreat practice; it becomes a way of living.[1]

At its heart, Ignatian spirituality is a *reflective* spirituality. We must *remember* if we are to stimulate our awareness of "patterns" in our experience. Ignatius himself becomes an exemplar of this learning process. He writes about his early spiritual experiences in his *Autobiography*.

> When he was thinking of those things of the world, he took much delight in them, but afterwards, when he was tired and put them aside, he found himself dry and dissatisfied. But when he thought of going to Jerusalem barefoot, and of eating nothing but plain vegetables and of practicing all the other rigors that he saw in the saints, not only was he consoled when he had these thoughts but even after putting them aside he remained satisfied and joyful.
>
> He did not notice this, however, nor did he stop to ponder the distinction until the time when his eyes were opened a little, and he began to marvel at the difference and to reflect upon it, realizing from experience that some thoughts left him sad and others joyful. Little by little he came to recognize the difference between the spirits that were stirring, the one from the devil, the other from God [8].

Ignatius describes some of his experiences as lasting over some period of time. But only after reflecting upon what had been happening to him does he come to perceive that the effects which some of these stirrings of the spirits have had upon him were different from the effects of others. Ignatius certainly believed in an external world of spirits, as is evidenced by the quotation above where he alludes to the devil and to God as the origins of the spirits moving him. And so it seems clear from this same text, as well as

---

[1] A version of this chapter was published in the Indian Jesuit journal *Ignis* (27 [1998], no. 3:3-10) and, in a much abbreviated form, in the American Jesuit (Missouri Province) publication *Jesuit Bulletin* as "Growing as a Contemplative in Action: Part Two, Contemplation and Discernment" (80, no. 3 [Fall 2001]: 12-13).

from other writings, that Ignatius uses the word *spirits* to refer also to the movements or motions that we feel interiorly. Our discerning—our discriminating the movements according to their different sources—has an eye to the direction these movements give to our life. This "noting" by Ignatius of the different deep feelings within his being provides him with the beginnings of what will come to be formulated as his *reglas* (guides, guidelines, norms) for discernment.

Ignatius's Gift of Guidelines

Although discernment as a special spiritual gift to individuals is present in the Hebrew Scriptures, St. Paul names and identifies this gift of the Spirit as a special charism within the whole Christian community. Ignatius takes his place in a long list of men and women who have contributed to a greater understanding and exercise of this charism or grace of discernment. When we are *discerning*, we are evaluating interior movements and discriminating between what is "of God" from what is "not of God." For Ignatius, discernment looks more to the heart than to the head for its effectiveness.

From his own experience with God and from his working with others, Ignatius developed in the Exercises two sets of *reglas*—guides, guidelines, norms—for our discerning process. These *reglas* or guidelines are considered classic in the spiritual tradition of the church. They were written with regard to the interior movements commonly encountered by people making the Exercises, but they are not restricted to this situation. As Ignatius describes them, the first set of guidelines is more suitable to the First Week experience (where evil wears little disguise and where good is made visible), and the second set is more subtle (where the apparent good turns out bad and where good seems immeasurable) and more applicable to the experiences common to the Second, Third, and Fourth Weeks. There is never a time, however, when we do not need to be helped by both sets of guidelines.

As Jules Toner, SJ, emphasized in his thorough study of Ignatian discernment, discernment is not primarily focused on choice or decision making.[2] Discernment deals always with relationship. From the etymology

---

[2] See Jules Toner, SJ, *A Commentary on Saint Ignatius's Rules for the Discernment of Spirits: A Guide to the Principles and Practice* (St. Louis: Institute of Jesuit Sources, 1982). This book acts as the necessary predecessor of his *Discerning God's Will: Ignatius of Loyola's Teaching on Christian Decision-*

of the word, we know that *discernment* refers to a way of "seeing," a way of orienting oneself, and also a way of "coming to a decision"—and, for us Christians, *in relation to* Christ (God). For Ignatius, imagination and contemplation are integral to discernment. We know from the Ignatian vision structures, such as the Principle and Foundation, that we live in a world permeated by God. We know also that God wants to be in relationship with us through all his gifts of creation. Jesus clarified the notion of this relationship by his call to us to be his disciples, his followers. From the Second Week on, the Exercises have provided us with a special experience of praying the Gospels, a privileged way of "putting on the mind of Christ." The Ignatian discernment strategy has its roots in the contemplation strategy of a docile awareness. Ignatian contemplation makes us so attentive to Jesus that we absorb his way of seeing, his way of responding, his sensitivity to the One he calls Abba, Father, and his way of choosing and deciding in the light of this relationship. In the Exercises, it is through contemplating the Gospel mysteries that we find ourselves coming to know Jesus. So, as we are shaped and formed by this relationship in the course of our praying, we find it increasingly easier to *feel* which choice or decision in our own life holds us close to Jesus and which one seems to lead us away from Jesus.

Ignatius passed on to us the fruits of his experience of paying attention to the deep motions within his own spirit. As he examined these movements and attended to the kind of direction that they gave to his life, he began to see these movements as a way in which God was communicating with him. So thoughts, imaginings, desires, loves, fears, affective feelings, impulses, inclinations such as peace, coldness, consolation, desolation—everything that Ignatius referred to as *movements*—become guides or criteria for our differentiating between the lead of God or the good spirit and the lead of the devil or the evil spirit in deciding the direction of our life. In Ignatian discernment, we are learning this new (for us) language of God.

Making (St. Louis: Institute of Jesuit Sources, 1991). Very helpful in clarifying and understanding these books are two practical application texts written by Toner: *Spirit of Light or Darkness? A Casebook for Studying Discernment of Spirits* (St. Louis: Institute of Jesuit Sources, 1995) and *What Is Your Will, O God? A Casebook for Studying Discernment of God's Will* (St. Louis: Institute of Jesuit Sources, 1995).

The Spectrum of Discernment

Discernment as applied to decision making might be seen more as a spectrum phenomenon than as a discrete or occasional process. There are definite periods in life when a specific decision or choice is called for, one that is life altering, that sets new directions. Then there is also a range of decisions or choices varying greatly in their importance to our relationship to God. As a result, the discernment process, as it is applied to decisions, changes in its time demands, personal effort, and intensity. When we have a decision to make, there is the possibility that in our process of discerning we can get caught up in an exclusive focus on the future. Ignatius carefully directs our attention to looking back so that we might look forward. It is by reflecting on our past experience and seeing how God has been active, or perhaps how we have ignored God, that we are sensitized to seeing the divinely patterned paths which lead over the horizon of our vision. For Ignatius, there is only one place for us to start in our discernment process: We must reflect on our past experience and trace the patterns of God in our life. In fact, for Ignatius the daily examen was a continual check on our "discerning" way of living. The examen, because of its "dailyness," is basic to our living as discerning people.

The Ignatian strategy of discernment is a process as clearly and distinctly structured as the three times of decision making identified in the Exercises. It is also a process of becoming sensitive to God that is as instinctive and commonplace—almost spontaneous—as we experience in the daily consciousness examen. Ignatian discernment holds us to the Christian belief that God does move our hearts and that we can grow daily in our sensitivity as lovers responding to God. Because of our sensitizing love, we experience that our choices and decisions are beyond the rational or reasonable. Often we limit discernment to the three-step process of the listing of pros and cons on a sheet of paper, then to praying about the matter, and finally coming to a decision with the expectation of experiencing a sense of peace. Ignatius identifies a "third time" of choice or decision making that involves this kind of reasoning process [177, 178]. He suggests that we make use of this method when we do find that the previous two "times" have not given us any results [175, 176]. At the same time, Ignatius always directs us to pray that God give us confirmation according to the affective experiences of the second or first times. Discernment is being able to listen and respond to the language of God spoken within our hearts and expressed in our affections. In the Ignatian pedagogy, we need to pay attention to and carefully evaluate the movement within our affections—much as Ignatius describes his reflections and things learned in his *Autobiography*. As Pascal states in his wisdom saying, "The heart has its reasons."

We remember that Ignatius presents the first time of election or choice as one in which we experience a constant clarity of direction or decision that God by his grace provides us. Although Ignatius refers to the dramatic conversion of Saul the persecutor to Paul the missionary apostle and to the abrupt call of Levi the tax collector to Matthew the apostle-evangelist as two examples of this first-time discernment, some commentators caution us not to focus on the seemingly extraordinary events surrounding their conversions, but rather to look to the constant sense of call or decision in their lives. Probably we would find this sense of call or inclination not so rare or unusual in our own life. Provided that we are not people who are always absolutely sure and clear about our decisions and directions (this might indicate more a self-assured person's presumption or pride than true discernment), there are times when what we are to do or what direction we are to take seems to rise up inside us with constant clarity. In his *Autobiography* [27], Ignatius gives the example of his own decision to eat meat after abstaining from it for some time. For Ignatius, this is God's Spirit working within us in a first-time discernment. Our response is to thank God and to offer the decision or choice to God as part of our loving service and then to act on it.

Discernment and Christ

Working with the second-time discernment is a unique contribution of Ignatius. It is based on our sensitivity to the movements that go on within our spirit. Ignatius calls these movements "spirits" and we feel the effect of these spirits in our affections. Our affections, or what we commonly call our feelings, provide us with a sense of spiritual consolation or spiritual desolation. We must carefully attend to the consolation and desolation Ignatius describes as *spiritual* [316, 317] if we are to become discerning people. Movements result in affections that may either excite and strengthen us in our following of Christ or lead us to darkness and discouragement. Being able to discern the spirits through our sensitivity to the affections being stirred in us is what the second-time discernment is all about.

Discernment, especially through consolation and desolation movements, is tied closely to the contemplations of the Exercises. Ignatius intends that, through contemplations on the Gospel mysteries, we observe Jesus so closely that we absorb, not only how he responds to people and events, but also how he comes to decisions and choices. It is as if Jesus is mentoring us. It is his example we internalize, even more than any teaching provided or directions given. Our absorbing Jesus' way of discerning is all part of the "following" which goes along with the "knowing intimately" and the "loving more" that is the grace we pray for in the Exercises from the Second Week on. To look at it in another perspective, we love Jesus as the well center of our life, and our discerning of choices and directions always dips back into that centering relationship. The disturbance of desolation happens because our movement is away from Jesus. The deepening of faith, hope, and love as a consolation movement happens because we are enhancing our relationship with Jesus.

The second-time discernment, then, is intimately interwoven with imagination and contemplation. For Ignatius, the way of Gospel contemplation is all of a piece with becoming discerning people. The intimacy with Christ that this kind of imaginative entering into the Gospel scene allows provides us not only with the "feel" of discernment in Jesus' life, but also with the realization that our love relationship with Jesus makes him the true norm of our discernment. Discernment in any of the three times demands a certain amount of imagination since we are dealing with "possibles" and "futurables"—and not just working with facts and figures and what is. We need to trust our imagination as a way that we allow God to be creative in communicating with us.

For us to be contemplatives in action means that we are also to be discerning people. A "contemplative" is one who is somehow in touch with God. A contemplative "in action" is one who in all the choices and decisions of everyday living is caught up always in their relationship with God. If we are in contact with God while we continue to make our choices and decisions, we are known as discerning people. We may not have consciously put the two together in this way, but we find discerning people and contemplatives in action are the same. Although the head is used in both contemplation and discernment, the emphasis in entering into the activity is on the heart. Discernment and contemplation are not a "some time" activity, but rather a quality of heartfelt living that we strive to deepen by God's grace as we grow in Ignatian spirituality.

Chapter Sixteen

REGLAS: GUIDELINES AND MODELS

In the text of the *Spiritual Exercises* book, Ignatius presents us with five sets of *reglas* (guides/guidelines, norms, models, frames/frameworks, literally "rules"). At the end of the Third Week, we meet the first set of *reglas*, those that deal with regulating our current eating and drinking habits for future health benefits (physical and spiritual) [210]. Then, added to the text of the Fourth Week exercises, but apparently outside of the retreat proper, are the four other sets of Ignatian *reglas*. There are two sets regarding discernment: (1) *reglas* for somehow perceiving and knowing the different movements that are caused in the soul [313ff.]; and (2) *reglas* for achieving the same result but with greater discernment of spirits [328ff.]. Ignatius also contributes *reglas* or guidelines to be observed in the ministry of distributing alms [337ff.]. His *Spiritual Exercises* book closes with *reglas* to be observed if we are to have the true sentiment that we ought to have in the church militant [352ff.].

It has been an esteemed tradition to show respect for venerable Christian texts by translating them into rather literal English, thus preserving the letter, if not always the spirit and intent, of the original text. Consequently, to avoid practicing—and teaching others—an uninformed, fundamentalist understanding of translated Christian texts, it is helpful, first, to bear in mind that what we are reading is indeed a translation, likely a rather literal translation, and second, to consult appropriate commentaries and other translations for a clearer understanding of the original.

In the case of the *Spiritual Exercises* book, most English versions commonly translate the broader, more general Spanish word *regla(s)* with the narrower, more specific word "rule(s)," regardless of context and connotation. However, the twenty-first century reader of Ignatius's book most often sees and hears the word "rules" in the context of a specific game or place in which particular actions are prescribed or proscribed as necessary conditions for achieving or avoiding/preventing a particular consequence— for instance, a baseball rule requires the home-run hitter to sequentially touch or "tag" the first, second, and third bases as well as home plate in order to score a run (earn a point) and avoid being "out"; a school rule against copying from other students' exams must be observed both to avoid the penalty of a failing grade and to have the possibility of earning a passing grade. Naturally, then, the contemporary reader of translated Ignatian texts is inclined to understand all uses of "rules" in the same particular, prescriptive, absolute sense of *do's* and *don'ts*—"do this or else" or "don't do this or else." But Ignatius's use of the Spanish word *regla(s)* throughout the text of his *Spiritual Exercises* is different. Though based on the same original metaphor of the carpenter's straight-edged tool (Latin "regula," Spanish "regla," English "rule" or "ruler"), the Ignatian meaning is more general, descriptive, and relative, referring to general aspects of thought, feeling, and attitude rather than to particular actions. Accordingly, the Ignatian term *reglas* (translated literally as "rules") is better understood and translated as "guides/guidelines," "norms," "models," or "frames/frameworks"— depending on the context—because Ignatius meant for us to receive them, not as *do's* or *don'ts*, but as helps and guidelines in setting parameters and frames for our personal growth and development. As Ignatius notes in one of his *reglas* for distributing alms [344], Christ is above all our *regla*, that is, our model and our guide.

Ignatian Uses of *Reglas*

This kind of personal reference for the word *regla(s)* is found also in Ignatius's second way of making a good and sound election [184ff.] within the third time. Whereas in the first way in this third time (this first way being of a more reasoned approach to discernment) there are six *punctos* or "points" [178ff.], in the second way Ignatius carefully notes that there are four *reglas* or "guidelines" [184ff.]. *Punctos* or "points," as we know from the prayer exercises, refer to content and provide the material with its particular focus about which we actively engage. "Points," as in the expression "points for discussion," refer to something we do. *Reglas,* on the other hand, refer more to parameters of activity and provide us not so much with content as with the frame or framework within which we act.

The first *regla*, "guideline" or "framework," that Ignatius draws our attention to is love—the love which moves us and makes us choose is focused always on God, our Creator and Lord [184]. This reference to the Principle and Foundations reminds us again how this first exercise "frames" every exercise of the retreat. The frame is not some commandment or some imperative word, but the face of a personal, loving God. The second *regla* proposes that we consider our own advice to someone unknown to us but for whom we want the best; then take the advice we give that other person and apply it to ourselves [185]. And so we "see" our life through the personal framing of another's life decision.

The third Ignatian *regla,* "guideline or frame," has us imagine ourselves looking back from a future time when we are at death's door, has us consider what method and norms we would wish we had used to make the decision of that earlier time, and has us then from that perspective make the present decision using those norms [186]. In a similar way, the fourth *regla* has us image ourselves on the day of judgment standing before God, next consider what norms we would then wish we had observed in making our present decision, and finally use those very norms to make the decision at hand so that we may find ourselves in the fullness of joy [187].

Obviously both the third and fourth *reglas* or frames come from our own personal imaging of the objective reality of our decision and its effect, and then acting decisively *now* from what we have imaginatively seen. In an added note, Ignatius points out that, when we apply these *reglas* aimed at our eternal salvation and peace, we give a proper framing to our matters of choice [188]. Now we are enabled to make our election and offer it to God our Lord, and we must beg that God's confirmation will be expressed through the graced experience of spiritual consolation.

To gain further clarity on Ignatius's use of the Spanish word *regla* (guideline, norm, model), we should also note its application in his Three Methods of Prayer [238]. Ignatius uses *regla* a number of times in the description of prayer methods that he locates after the Fourth Week exercises. The first usage is in Ignatius's attempt to give a guideline or norm for the length of time we reflect on each commandment, thinking of how we have kept it and in what ways we have failed [241]. He suggests that we observe the *regla* of spending the space of time it takes to say three Our Fathers and three Hail Marys. The amount of time suggested here is not really a rule for a set number of minutes, but rather a guideline for a period of time to be spent, expressed in the phrase "taking about so much time." Ignatius repeats this same idea of *regla* in two other sections [244, 246]. He has a similar use in his points on rhythmic prayer [258-260]. After describing how one word of a prayer formula, such as *Father* in the Our Father would be said between one breath and the next, Ignatius then goes on to say that, in the whole time from one breath to the next, attention should be given chiefly to the meaning of this word or to the person to whom we recite it and so on. This description becomes the guideline or model for all the other words of the familiar vocal prayer being used [258].

Ignatius next gives two *reglas* (guidelines or models) to be followed in this Third Method of Prayer. The first *regla* is to use other vocal prayers, such as the Hail Mary, in the rhythmic way of praying that was just described for the Our Father [259]. That description becomes our model for this way of praying any of the prayers we know. The second *regla* expands the notion of praying any one prayer to allowing a rhythmic way of praying a variety of prayers or parts of prayers in a single period [260]. Again we are presented with a guideline, a model for adapting a way of praying with which we have become familiar.

More generally, we might note that Ignatius adds this section about the Three Methods of Prayer as a help for the director and retreatant so that the consistency of a prayer life can be maintained after the retreat. Prayer need not require books or a Bible or a director—none of which was easily available in Ignatius's day. These helps are meant to be freeing and supportive for the retreatant looking towards the time after the retreat. Even with the abundance of prayer material today, the Ignatian addition of these prayer notes immediately after the last exercise of the Fourth Week reminds directors in every age that they need to make suggestions and give support for the life of prayer after the retreat.

Reglas or Guidelines for Eating

Let us look now at each of the sets of *reglas* or guidelines that are a part of the *Spiritual Exercises* book. The guidelines for eating that come at the conclusion of the Third Week have provoked a lot of speculation [210ff.]. Why does Ignatius single out a special set of guidelines just for eating? Why would eating be placed in the Third Week? What does the added phrase "for the future" point to—the rest of the Third Week, or just the Fourth Week and/or the time after the retreat?

Since the notes which make up the Exercises were corrected and nuanced by Ignatius for over twenty years until the first printing of the *Spiritual Exercises* book in 1548, it does not seem likely that the placement of the guidelines for eating in its position at the Third Week's close is a happenstance. It is not too farfetched to think that the foundational position of the Last Supper contemplation at the beginning of the Week would stimulate a reflection on eating. More basically, we might ask ourselves what would move Ignatius to take up the giving of guidelines for the activity of eating. We know that he ruined his own health by the extremes in diet that he had taken on early in his attempt to live a serious penitential life. As a good director, he may have wanted to impart some practical guidelines about eating to people newly fired up in their spiritual life by the Exercises. It is a positive way for Ignatius to say, "Learn from my mistakes." He had already, within the First Week's material, given some guidelines on eating in connection with penance, but he is now looking at the everyday activity of food consumption as regards a person renewed in his or her following of Christ.

Besides the practical help that the Exercises were meant to provide for someone making a life decision or reforming a life already chosen, Ignatius intended that the Exercises would affect our ordinary way of living. The daily examen is an obvious example of how a prayer period is meant to be built into our ordinary day-to-day life. I believe that Ignatius takes up the human activity of eating because, again, it is a daily activity. Through the Exercises we have prayed to put on "the mind of Christ." We have watched Jesus in all his ordinary activities, including his being present and eating at banquets. Ignatius's *reglas* or guidelines are presented for us to use either in themselves or as a model for forming our own guidelines so that when we eat or drink—whatever we do—we do it in Christ Jesus, as St. Paul says. The Exercises-graced decision to live differently because of our closeness to Christ can be practically applied to eating as to every other daily activity of life. Ignatius's guidelines for eating, then, not only provide norms for this daily activity, but also become a model for any number of other guidelines that we might find helpful to draw up for ordinary activities seen as affecting our relationship with Christ. As a matter of fact, Ignatius himself in his role as superior general of the newly founded Society of Jesus wrote (and had others help write) similar short practical guidelines for different aspects of community living, especially guidelines for those who held positions of responsibility for others.

The phrase "for the future" may well look to how we will begin to implement our resolves about eating even as we move into the Fourth Week. But it seems obvious that the direction indicated is more largely understood to refer to the ordinary time after the retreat has been completed. Just as the retreatant is given greater latitude in personally adapting prayer in the Third and Fourth Weeks, so Ignatius also suggests through his guidelines for eating that we need to set ourselves ways to bring the graces of the retreat into the practical details of our life. He intends that, in the midst of carrying out our life-direction decision or our reformation of life, we are realizing objective ways of incarnating our new Christ relationship in everyday life.

Positioning this set of *reglas* or guidelines within the retreat proper would indicate that Ignatius expects retreatants to consider how they are going to implement such practical guidelines in their daily life. We may well start making these guidelines part of our daily living even in the final days of the retreat. While the guidelines for eating may serve as a model for the practical guidelines for every other activity that enhances our relationship with Jesus, this very set of guidelines has universal application since all of us have to take nourishment. None of the other sets of Ignatian *reglas* or guidelines applies so universally, and so Ignatius writes them as an addition to the text of the Exercises. The position of these other guidelines at the end of the text indicates that they may not be presumed to be helpful or applicable to everyone making the Exercises. But Ignatius shows his concern for retreatants with more specialized responsibilities by his careful crafting of guidelines that might help them live the graces of the Exercises.

Reglas or Guidelines for the Ministry of Almsgiving

In continuing to encourage practical steps that implement the life changes that the retreat grace has brought about, Ignatius adds a set of *reglas* or guidelines dealing with a particular ministry in the church—the ministry of almsgiving [337ff.]. In Ignatius's day, with no government social agencies to look after the poor and disabled, only the institutional church, through sharing the gifts of its benefices (loosely speaking, the equivalent of our modern-day foundations that share their endowment profits), looked after those in need. Some people, both clerical and lay, inherited or were given the responsibility to distribute to those in need the profits from the benefices that had been established. Since they were laboring in a charitable work in the name of the church, they were exercising a true ministry. In Ignatius's day, as often happens when dealing with money resources, there were abuses—with those in charge of benefices using the resources for themselves and their family members, with cases of bribery on the part of the recipients, and so on. Ignatius wants to present guidelines for people exercising this charitable ministry. It is within these guidelines that he names Christ—under the Letter to the Hebrews title of High Priest (so denoting a ministerial role)—as our one *regla*, guide or model [344]. Of course, Christ is always *the* guide and model for all the Ignatian *reglas,* but this is the only set of *reglas* in which Ignatius makes it explicit. Although this *regla* comes last in this set, it is obviously the foundational principle for all the preceding *reglas.* For Ignatius, this set of *reglas* itself serves as a model that could be adapted to any service, work, or ministry. Even if this set of guidelinesdid not apply to a particular retreatant, Ignatius's concern was again that some retreatants would be helped to draw up similar guidelines, practically spelled out for their own work or ministry, in order to better live out the grace of the retreat.

Reglas or Guidelines for Thinking with the Church

Ignatius is also famous for his *reglas* or guidelines for thinking with the church [352ff.]. With his expectation that a number of the people who will have made the Exercises will be taking a more active role in living their Catholic life, Ignatius wishes to help prepare them to face life in the everyday church after the divine-hothouse atmosphere of the retreat. He carefully chooses the noun *sentido,* from the verb *sentir* ("to have a heartfelt response"), to be a part of the original Spanish title for this set of *reglas. Sentir* connotes both a rational and an affective approach, a kind of thinking that resonates with one's whole being.[1] The action of *sentir* is associated with a discerning person whose "heart has its reasons." Ignatius consistently links affections and discernment with a *sentir* approach to our spiritual life. His *reglas* or norms for thinking with the church are no exception. Ignatius is not one to hold up as an ideal the approach of "you command, I obey." The obedience for which his Society of Jesus came to be known was a *holy* obedience, *holy* only if the parties involved were discerning people. In his guidelines for having the true sentiment *(sentido)* that we should in the church militant, he presents the same ideal. He knows that a person stepping forward for active involvement in church life needs practical, helpful guidelines to keep working daily at a discerned way of living such service.

---

[1] See George Ganss, SJ, *The Spiritual Exercises of Saint Ignatius: A Translation and Commentary* (St. Louis: Institute of Jesuit Sources, 1992), 199, #164.

Ignatius wants to provide guidelines (or a model for drawing up one's own guidelines) that help a person who is living a new relationship with Christ to resonate with church-life beliefs and practices. For Ignatius, the first of these *reglas* or guidelines expresses how important it is for our inside feelings and attitudes to be one with our outside behavior and activity if we want to live a true sentiment (*sentido*) in keeping with the policies and practices of the church. The first guideline serves as a sort of foundational principle for the rest of the guidelines in this set. The church is warmly described in personal terms as "the true spouse of Christ our Lord" and "our holy mother the church." Then Ignatius adds a more institutional element with the expression "the church hierarchical" [353] (perhaps a description original with him) in order to make sure that we are identifying *this* church that we love with the visible institutional church centered in Rome, focused in our parish church, and expressed in the persons of bishops, priests, religious, and laity who are its members.

As Ignatius spells out the rest of the *reglas* or guidelines in this set, we are made aware of the "practical" application of such guidelines. What is reflected in their content and in the way that such *reglas* or norms are expressed is the kind of difficulties and contentions existing in the church just at the time it was looking towards its Council of Trent reforms. In these *reglas*, Ignatius expresses concern for living faithfully in three areas of our church life: observing worship, dealing with authorities, and evaluating preaching and teaching. In keeping with his Presupposition [22] at the beginning of the *Spiritual Exercises* book, Ignatius stresses the necessity of a positive attitude, which often requires great personal effort whenever we approach any of these areas of church life. We seek to understand rather than to condemn, we favor the better interpretation, and we respect and use the proper channels of redress.

As in the case of the *reglas* for the ministry of almsgiving, the *reglas* for thinking with the church have great importance for retreatants today, but much more as general "models" for how to formulate practical, here-and-now guidelines than as guidelines to be directly applied in the same specific form that Ignatius presented them. What has not lost its relevance is the areas of modeling which these *reglas* represent for one growing in his or her Christ identity.

Reglas or Guidelines for Discernment

The two sets of *reglas* or guidelines for discernment both fit with what we have been saying about the Ignatian use of guidelines in general, and yet they each have at the same time their own uniqueness [313ff. and 328ff.]. Like the two previous sets of guidelines, for the ministry of almsgiving and for thinking with the church, both sets of guidelines for discernment are located outside of the retreat proper. In the annotations at the beginning of the *Spiritual Exercises* book, Ignatius has prepared us for this placement. In the Eighth and Ninth Annotations he has carefully instructed the director to explain the *reglas* or guidelines for the First and Second Weeks insofar as the retreatant needs and would find helpful such an explanation. But he quickly warns the director not to explain too much, especially if one or other guideline should be too subtle or too advanced. Ignatius, then, sees that not every retreatant would need to know the whole of either of the two sets of guidelines. Here, above all, Ignatius instructs the director: use whatever helps.

Without repeating what we have said about discernment in the previous chapter, we should mention that what seems unique about these *reglas* or guidelines is that Ignatius does not set them up as a model from which other people can draw up their own particular guidelines. The guidelines for discernment, while still guidelines, fit more the designation of "wisdom teachings." From the fact that these Ignatian guidelines are truly guidelines, we conclude that the director and retreatant are being given parameters helpful for understanding the movements of the spirits and for taking appropriate action. They are both enabled to act wisely. Because the very application of the discernment guidelines requires discernment on the part of those working with them, Ignatius indicates that the guidelines he has given are the ones that are helpful in themselves. These *reglas* or guidelines hold their wisdom within themselves. As a result, Ignatius gives no indication that retreatants could or should be encouraged to draw up their own guidelines for discernment. Perhaps Ignatius thinks that the subtlety of discernment requires a person already long experienced in being taught by God, just as Ignatius felt that he himself had been taught over a long period of time and needed that much time in order to learn.

Discernment as part of wisdom is intimately connected with the Ignatian idea of devotion. As described in his *Autobiography* [99], devotion for Ignatius is an ease in finding God. Devotion relates to discernment because discernment refers to a way of communicating easily between God and human beings. Discernment needs to be seen as analogous to various other ways we have of communicating. We know the differences between oral and written communications, between philosophical and scientific forms of expression, and between different kinds of computer languages. We are aware of special language communications between friends and lovers. In every example, there is a learning process, a development of skill, and often a working through of miscommunications and of missed signals. Marriage counseling often deals with this kind of communication difficulty.

From his experience, Ignatius tries to set down some guidelines to help us in our learning process. But always he presumes the loving relationship between God and the human being (the retreatant). Because God is always trying to communicate with us, as we know from the Principle and Foundation, it is up to us to be able to hear and understand the language of God. However, discernment is not, strictly speaking, just a technique to be learned; rather, because we are growing in the ease with which we find God in all things, discernment includes the God-given grace of responding to God's communication. Discernment deals with the language of lovers. When we enter into discernment, we are not talking simply about knowledge; we are speaking of wisdom.

Notes on Scruples

Ignatius has one other addition to his Exercises besides the four sets of *reglas* or guidelines. This addition he simply entitles *Notas* ("Notes") [345ff.]. These notes deal with recognizing and understanding scruples—an affliction that Ignatius experienced, especially in his early years of conversion. Ignatius apparently wrote these notes early in the composition of the Exercises. He seems to have thought that they could be helpful to certain retreatants who might suffer from similar problems. But he makes the decision not to call them *reglas* or guidelines inasmuch as they do not provide the wisdom guidelines of discernment or the practical guidelines that might model one's own way of proceeding in following Christ. But Ignatius does share from his experience what he has found helpful, and so we are presented with a few things "to be noted."

It seems a large number of retreatants, untroubled by scruples, would have little reason to "note" these reflections by Ignatius. Likewise, Ignatius does not seem to have thought he had written something like a guideline, which could be used as a frame or model similar to his other (earlier) guidelines. For he gives no indication that he would expect people to find his notes a model for drawing up their own guidelines for a way of living.

The great merit in all of the Ignatian *reglas* or guidelines lies in their dynamic quality. These are living guidelines in that they are guiding principles whose aim is their practical application to our Christian living. They truly give us guidelines and models for our continuing growth in Christ.

Chapter Seventeen

IGNATIAN SPIRITUALITY: A WAY
OF PROCEEDING

Ignatian spirituality is sometimes called "a spirituality for busy people."[1] Sometimes it is identified as a "worldly spirituality." At other times it is described as a "world-affirming spirituality."

It is helpful if we have a common understanding of what we mean by *spirituality*. Simply said, spirituality is "a way of living." In our Christian context we fill out our description by adding "influenced by the Gospels and Jesus' gift of the Spirit." In a slightly more technical description, we might say that spirituality deals with a faith vision (a way of seeing), its articulation, and its application to our everyday life with God, with neighbor, and with the world.

How do we come to live a Christian spirituality which is identified with Ignatius Loyola—through his way of seeing God, neighbor, and world?

Most adults develop new or different ways of seeing from another person's sharing of a viewpoint. In terms of a religious or faith vision, it may happen when we hear a homily or when we read an article or a book. An influential teacher can share a vision of life, or a good friend may share deeply and effectively in a seemingly simple conversation. Ignatius Loyola shared his faith vision in his classic retreat manual called *Spiritual Exercises* and in his religious-life rule called *Constitutions of the Society of Jesus*. Ignatius often made use of an expression—"our way of proceeding"—when he laid down a rule of life for the religious group called the Society of Jesus. If we expand the application of this expression beyond Jesuit life, we observe that there is a way of proceeding, a way of going about life, a faith-

---

[1] The ideas presented in this chapter were first published in the Indian journal *Ignis* (28, no. 2 (1999): 3-12). In a similar way, these ideas were later published as an article in three parts, "How Do We Live an Ignatian Spirituality?" (*Jesuit Bulletin* 79, no. 1 [Winter]: 12-13, no. 2 [Spring/Summer]: 12-13, and no. 3 [Fall 2000]: 12-13, respectively).

oriented way of seeing and entering into relationship with our world which can be described as Ignatian.

It is obvious that we are not talking about some pious practices or set devotions. Rather, Ignatian spirituality is a matter of basic attitudes, ways of relating to Jesus and God the Father and the Spirit, with certain values emphasized, and with our human involvement in the work of the kingdom, the reign of God.

What are some of the pieces that make up the way of proceeding that we identify as Ignatian spirituality? Perhaps we could sum them up under the following headings.

A Media God

For Ignatius Loyola, our God is a God who wants to break into our life through even more channels than our cable television set has.

Today we are conscious of the importance of the media—usually meaning newspapers, television, radio, movies, and now computers with access to the internet and email. Ignatius, without any foreknowledge of our modern sense of the media, imagined God as breaking into our life in a myriad of ways everyday. Through people and events, through our own interior moods and affections, through the Scriptures, and through our prayer, God is trying to communicate with us.

We may have had the experience of observing a monolingual person trying to communicate with someone who does not understand his language. Since the monolingual person has had communication problems only with the hard of hearing, he typically has the tendency to speak louder as if there is a hearing problem rather than a language problem. This may serve as an analogy for how we pray to God. Sometimes we scream out in "our" language of request, asking for, perhaps demanding, things we want. All the while God is trying to respond and we do not even listen to, or try to understand, God's language.

Ignatius tries to get us to be more aware of how God wants to enter into our everyday life. If, for Ignatius, God is a media God, then the following component is integral to Ignatian spirituality.

Human Experience and Reflection

Ignatius wants to expand our view of the world from the narrow medium of an 8mm, black-and-white, silent movie to a panoramic screen of full-color richness, with sound and music. He presents a picture of creation—expressed succinctly in the Principle and Foundation and in the Contemplation on the Love of God in his retreat manual *Spiritual Exercises*—which makes us more conscious of the many levels and layers of our experience in our daily work-a-day world. Our problem as people of faith is not that God is absent from our life and world. It is, rather, that we are so busy, so self-focused, that we do not give God a thought. Even our regular Sunday Mass experience—meant to be a special "Sabbath" celebration with God—can become more a formalized ritual and less a reflective, human experience.

Ignatius was in synch with how the Israelites, when reflecting or looking back on their experience, saw how God had been continuously present to them and had guided and comforted them in good times and in bad. Ignatius reflected on his own experience, his dreams and desires, and began to discover how God and God's desires became more apparent to him in the events of his life. An essential aspect of Ignatian spirituality is a view of God as One who comes in many ways into our life—a multimedia God. That is the kind of Christian God we come to know—through a sensitized awareness. But the concomitant aspect is regular reflection on our daily experience. Experiential awareness and reflection on our experience are central to our growth in being able to hear and being able to respond to the language of God—to the God who struggles to communicate with us.

To Know Christ Jesus: Laboring

We often use the expression "media event" when we refer to a major newsworthy happening. The "media event" of our Christian God is "God becoming incarnate," the person of Jesus Christ, acknowledged as Son of God, our Savior.

Ignatius suggests in his *Spiritual Exercises* that we picture the three Persons of our triune God looking from above on the human scene on planet earth—much as we gaze at the evening world news on TV—and that we then observe how they engage in conversation about what could be done to heal and right our human situation. Our triune God makes a choice to enter into the messiness of human living, even into its most unfair, cruel, and death-dealing aspects. The divine decision is that the second Person will become incarnate—begging permission from the virgin Mary to do so and waiting upon her *fiat* ("let it be done"). And so Jesus is born of poor parents in an occupied land and knows the experience of living as a refugee.

Ignatius has a "way of proceeding" by which we cancome to know and love and follow Jesus: it is to enter with careful attention into the Gospel presentation of how Jesus acts and goes about life. We follow the same pattern for growing in our relationship with Jesus that all his disciples have followed since the first apostles responded to his call. Ignatius does not preach or draw moral examples from the Gospels. He puts us in prayer contact with the Gospels and has us enter as fully as we can into each scene—each Gospel event becoming so alive as we recreate it in imagination that we can truly enter into the scene and be present to the people involved. In this way of praying—called Ignatian contemplation—we drink in how Jesus looks, how he listens, how he speaks, how he acts. We learn much also from our taking in how other people in the Gospel incident interact with and respond to Jesus.

To live, St. Paul says, is "to know Christ Jesus." And Jesus says to Philip, "Philip, if you have seen me, you have seen the Father." How do we come to know Jesus, and so come to know God? For Ignatius, the one who drinks in Jesus will begin to live the way that God's children live—the way that the Son of God lives, the One who calls God Abba, Father.

A Spanish word that takes on divine meaning for Ignatius is *laborar* ("to labor" or "to work"). As Ignatius envisioned the Trinity, it was a labor of the Trinity to enter into the salvation of humankind: "Let us work the redemption of the human race" [107]. From the very beginning of Jesus' life, labor was involved—no room for them in the inn, then an exile in Egypt. And the great work of redemption is accomplished by his suffering and death on the cross and his being raised by God. Jesus described his mission as a choice of labor: "My Father works, and I work" (Jn 5:17). What we begin to understand through Ignatian spirituality is that our God is a busy God. As with Jesus, our own busyness, our labor, is a point of contact with, not a cause of separation from, our God.

To Know Christ Jesus: Poor

Ignatius does more than just put us into contact with Jesus as the prime medium of our living like sons and daughters of a God we too call *Father*. In the way that Ignatius has carefully constructed his *Spiritual Exercises* book, he has given us his own gospel picture of Jesus. It may strike our ears as peculiar—sounding almost heretical at first—to hear that Ignatius gives us *his* gospel picture of Jesus. Yet *that* is what each of our four Gospels does. Each Gospel presents a picture of Jesus—according to either Matthew or Mark or Luke or John, or, perhaps more correctly, according to the memories of the early churches they each represent.

Ignatius consistently uses one adjective to describe Jesus. It is not any of the adjectives that mean "loving," "compassionate," "gentle," or "kingly"—as appropriate as any of those words would be. Ignatius has a clear predilection for the word *pobre*, meaning "poor." Ignatius seems at the same time to equate *poverty* with *humility*. *Humility* has its root in the Latin word *humus*, meaning "earth" or "ground." So, for example, when we use the expression that someone "has his feet on the ground," "is down to earth," or "is well grounded," we would be describing a "humble" person. For Ignatius, "truth" and the "true life" are intimately related to being humble since we are creatures created by God "out of the clay of the ground" (Gn 2:7). Jesus claims to be "the way, and the truth, and the life" (Jn 14:6), and Ignatius identifies Jesus as the exemplar of the "true life." But in speaking this way about living the truth or being humble, we also might well be using the word *poor*. As Ignatius sees Jesus, he is, above all, a poor man, a humble man, one who lives the truth of "being grounded." Why should this be so important?

Ignatius follows the inspiration of St. Paul, whose basic description of Jesus is rooted in the early Christian hymn he quotes in his letter to the Philippians: "He did not consider godliness something to cling to, but rather he emptied himself, taking on our human nature" (Phil 2:6-7). Jesus becomes poor in becoming incarnate—going from godliness to humanness, an emptying out. Jesus is born into poverty—beginning life in a stable manger, fleeing as a refugee to Egypt, returning to live a simple workman's life in Nazareth. Jesus chooses to be poor—led by the Spirit to be an itinerant preacher and teacher, having no wife or children, no place to call home. Jesus dies poor—stripped even of the clothes he wore, considered a criminal and an outcast, buried in another man's tomb. Above all, for Ignatius, Jesus is poor in that he has nothing to claim as his own—everything is gift, everything is given him by his Father, even what he is to say. So Jesus accepts that he is poor in himself—true humility—but rich in his gifts, especially in his identity of being the Son of God, and free in his sharing with us as brothers and sisters who in his name call upon God as "Our Father."

Jesus is free—he clings to nothing. He holds fast to nothing because everything is gift. Lovers share whatever they have with the ones they love. Jesus, THE gift of God's love, gives himself totally over to us, even allowing us to put him to death. He loves us *to the very end*, which means, paradoxically, that he loves us in such a way that even death presents no limit to his love. God raises him up as the incarnation and visible sacrament of God's invincible love. Through his death and resurrection Jesus gifts us with hope of risen life forever—a life of love with God. Although Ignatius closes a number of his letters with the expression "poor in goodness," the true paradox of Jesus' poverty/richness is caught in another closing expression of Ignatius, which reads "poor in Jesus."

A Spiritual Guide

Another aspect of Ignatian spirituality flows from how we relate to God and from the many ways in which God works with us. Just as God worked the redemption incarnately—employing human means to bring about a divine end, so Ignatius places great importance on our using a spiritual director or guide as the normal means for us to make progress in becoming holy and to grow continually in the following of Jesus.

A spiritual guide is like a mirror. We all can live without a mirror, but a mirror makes combing our hair and shaving or putting on makeup a lot easier. With a mirror, we do a better job of cleaning and grooming ourselves. In a similar way a spiritual director makes it easier to see better our interaction with God. It is not so much the wisdom or great insight that a particular guide may bring to that relationship with God. Rather, the importance of the guide is found in the careful listening and the "reflecting back" (a la a mirror) that helps us come to see how God is working in our life—how apparently disparate elements come together into some meaningful pattern—and helps us even to understand a little the kind of rhythm or pattern of interaction which God and we seem to embrace in our mutual relationship. For Ignatius, then, there is an importance of a human spiritual director or guide to keep us consistently alert to God's movements and to help us, in a discerning manner, interpret those movements for our continuing spiritual growth. It is with the aid of a spiritual guide that we learn ever better the "language of God" spoken through the various media that flood our life. The spiritual director is the one who enables us to grow as "discerning" persons—persons whose decisions or choices are made primarily with reference to a deepening relationship with God. "How does God want to work with us at this point in our individual lives?" and "What would God have us do now?" are our questions as discerning people. For Ignatius, a spiritual guide is always meant to be a helper, a mirror, an angel—a consistent medium through whom God works "sacramentally," a divine pattern that Christianity has come to embrace through Christ's command of sending forth apostles to act in his name.

Ministry and Mission

The final aspect of Ignatian spirituality flows from our active involvement with the God identified in Ignatian spirituality as a "media God." If God is coming into our individual lives in so many ways every day, we begin to realize that God is working through us in particular as one of his media to continue his work of bringing about the Kingdom. So what we do or do not do makes a difference in the way that God can break into his own created world. In a true sense God has made himself poor and dependent on us.

Ignatius describes us as *instruments*—a word which does not please our ears today in an age of personalism and individual rights. We ought not, however, lose the beautiful spiritual truth of the idea. Ignatius wanted people influenced by this "way of proceeding" in their Christian growth to realize the great glory of being an "instrument" in the hands of God. It was always an integral part of Ignatius's prayer to beg that God would use him, to work with and through him. If we live an Ignatian spirituality, we feel the pulse of God in our lives. We continue to desire to respond ever more wholeheartedly to the calls of God. We want to be an "instrument" in the hands of God. In Ignatian spirituality, as a result, mission or ministry—working with God—takes on certain characteristics.

The first signal for these particulars is given by the makeup of the *Spiritual Exercises* book. The book demands the involvement of the person making the Exercises, with the help of a director or guide. If we are influenced by Ignatian spirituality, then whatever our ministry, we do not simply do something *for* others, but we also interact *with* others in such a way that we involve those people in that very ministry. When parishes or retreat centers or social-work agencies are considered, *collaboration*—that is, working *together*, working *with* others—is the presumed "way of proceeding." Ministry demands teamwork, interaction with others. It is our faith vision that we make a difference. God desires that we make a difference as his collaborators in the Reign that God is here and now bringing about.

Finally, for us who try to live Ignatian spirituality, there is the deep-down desire to share our faith, to be evangelizers, and to witness by our lives to the Good News of Jesus Christ. Whatever be the ambit of our family and recreation and whatever be our line of work, we want Jesus to be central. We want Jesus to be known and to be just as real for others as he has become for us. We witness to our faith in the way we live and in the way we work. We witness to the person of Jesus and the meaning of his Gospel. We are the evangelizers whom Jesus has called "to make disciples of all nations." For in living Ignatian spirituality, we experience the Jesus who confirms "that I am with you always, until the end of the world" (Mt 28:20).

APPENDICES

Appendix One

The following essay was published in its original form in 1981 as an introduction to the book Notes on the Spiritual Exercises of St. Ignatius of Loyola *(St. Louis: Review for Religious, rev. 1983). I have made some adaptations of the text, but the key ideas remain unchanged. I have included this essay as an appendix since I believe that it serves well as a summary and a review of the major theme of all the preceding chapters of this book.*

THE IGNATIAN EXERCISES: UNDERSTANDING THEIR DYNAMICS

The book *Spiritual Exercises* by St. Ignatius Loyola has received many interpretations over the past four hundred years. Although these various studies are in their own ways good and helpful for a deeper understanding of his Exercises, I want to focus my own reflections upon the movement or dynamics presented by St. Ignatius. For the Ignatian gift to the retreat methods available within the church shines out in this special way: what characterizes every element in the Exercises is the sense of movement—described more fully as a movement forward as well as a movement in depth—toward a personal commitment to Jesus Christ.

Through a study of the history of spiritual developments within the church, we learn that there are many styles of retreats or what we might more generally describe as concentrated prayer periods or personal spiritual-renewal periods. We could set aside a certain number of days, for example, to center our prayer and our reading on the three theological virtues of faith, hope, and love. What results from this kind of retreat may be a greater personal understanding of these virtues, and perhaps some greater desire may be excited for integrating them more fully in our lives.

By contrast, Ignatius spent some twenty years constructing his book *Spiritual Exercises* so that it would embody a certain movement—what we traditionally call a "conversion experience." He found this movement or dynamics significant for his own commitment to Jesus Christ as well as for the commitment or conversion of many others with whom he worked. The movement involved these personal elements: a person going through these experiences (a retreatant), a person guiding them (a director), and God present to both persons. The Exercises themselves are focused primarily on passages from the four Gospels of Our Lord Jesus Christ, with certain key structures presented by Ignatius at precise intervals, usually as a distillation of the various call passages or teachings of Jesus within the Gospels. The carefully constructed flow of the Exercises was written down specifically as a help for the person giving them in order to facilitate the response to God's grace in an individual Christian's life.

A variety of words or expressions has been used to try to capture some central aspects of the Exercises. All of them are drawn in some way from the Ignatian text itself. "Spiritual freedom" is one important way of describing the experience brought about by the Exercises. "A process of ordering our life values" is another expression of the Exercises' dynamics. "Indifference" or "detachment" is sometimes seen as the permeating ingredient of a person's life if it has been influenced by the Exercises. "Putting on the mind of Christ or the ability to see and make decisions the way in which Jesus sees and makes decisions" is another way of capturing the new quality of life nurtured by the making of the Exercises. The common element in all these descriptive phrases is a sense of dynamism; that is, it is not so much a newness measured by some knowledge we have come to learn through the Exercises as it is an introduction into an abiding attitude towards life, an all-inclusive way of going about living that is summed up in the Ignatian expression "a way of proceeding."

From the outset of these reflections, I would like to offer one caution. What appears to be such a rigidly structured approach, so meticulously ordered in hours of prayer and self-examination, in positions for prayer, in the use of food, sleep, penances, and so on, can only be studied with comprehension by someone who has had the experience of making the Exercises. A study of the Exercises that is not grounded in a personal experience of them is akin to a blind person's Braille reading all about the color red. In both instances, there is a certain comprehension of the words and expressions used, but there is still no real experience of "seeing." My own reflections, then, presume that the reader has had an experience of the Exercises. Although many people have experienced the full Exercises of thirty days in a group style through a preached or guided presentation, I will be considering the text of Ignatius's *Spiritual Exercises* book as it is presented over a thirty-day period in a personally directed retreat. In this approach I include also the full Exercises given as a retreat in everyday life, though some major adaptations need to be acknowledged.

Influenced by Ignatius's own meticulousness in setting down the order of the elements which make up the text of his *Spiritual Exercises* book, I too will try to reflect an orderliness as I attempt to shed light on the flow of the contents of his book. In the text that follows, the numbers enclosed within brackets refer to the paragraph numbers found in most modern editions and translations of the original Spanish text, *Ejercicios Espirituales*.

1. The Prayer "Soul of Christ"

What we find printed first in the book is not a part, strictly speaking, of the Ignatian text. Ignatius Loyola has long been associated with the prayer "Soul of Christ," so much so that at times he has been identified as its author. We know that Ignatius did not formulate this prayer, but it was a great favorite of his and he referred to it expressly in the text of the Threefold Colloquy [63, 147] and in the Three Methods of Prayer [253, 258]. Although this prayer was not prefixed to either the original Spanish or the early Latin editions, there grew up within the first forty years a lasting, almost universal custom of including it in the printed text of the *Spiritual Exercises* book. In a true sense, we can say that the prayer is a summing up of the whole movement and overall dynamics of the Exercises in terms of their Christ-centeredness. The *Soul of Christ* focuses line by line on our identifying ever more fully with the person of Christ so that he really becomes our life—or, more accurately stated, we live only in him. This prayer, like the movement present in the Exercises themselves, centers us so much upon the person of Jesus Christ that, with St. Paul, we are meant to exclaim "the life I live now is not my own, Christ is living in me" (Gal 2:20a). It is because of this spirit, and Ignatius's own references to the prayer, that this formula has for so long taken its integral place within the book *Spiritual Exercises*.

2. Annotations or Helps

The Annotations [1-20], called "Some Preliminary Helps" in Fleming; "Introductory Observations" in Puhl; and "Introductory Explanations" in Ganss, introduce Ignatius's text as he perfected it for its first printing. These twenty observations of Ignatius, along with the various additions and notes that he suggests in accord with the content material of the various weeks, provide the basic directions for how to proceed in the giving of the retreat. Throughout the years, many books—some of the early ones were called "directories," or guidebooks, for (directing) the Spiritual Exercises—have been written to give further aid to the retreat director and to the retreatant. But Ignatius's own pithy observations within the text remain the most essential tool for the good progress of the retreat. Even when the Exercises are adapted to various styles (preached, group-sharing, personal) and to various time limits (three-day, eight-day, and so on), these observations maintain an essential place in accommodating and applying the movement of the Exercises to the individual or the group and to the situation.

The fact that we find these annotations or helps placed first in the *Spiritual Exercises* book stresses the overriding importance of adaptation. Ignatius intended that the Exercises which he presented to the church and to the Society of Jesus were to be only sketchy outlines always to be accommodated by the director to a particular retreatant [18]. In these first directions, then, we are always reminded that there is no such thing as a "pure" presentation of the Exercises. There is only the unique accommodation or adaptation of the movement of conversion to a particular retreatant. Since the true director of the retreat is God alone [15], the human director must try to remain his instrument. This he or she does by listening carefully to the retreatant in the review of a retreat day and then proceeding to follow out the lead of the Spirit as best he or she can by the suggestions of such exercises as will further the movement of conversion. The Ignatian retreat director, as a result, cannot be caught up in a lock-step presentation of a text. The same kind of freedom is demanded of the retreat director as is sought by the retreatant through the methodology of the Exercises.

What promotes this kind of freedom of movement is found especially in the proper application of Ignatius's *reglas* or guidelines for the discernment of spirits [313-336], as he himself suggests in [8]. These reflections of Ignatius encapsulate for the director some guides or norms for observing and dealing with the spiritual forces in our lives that tend to lead us towards God or away from him. The more a director is listening and helping a person to become more adept at making use of the means which these guidelines provide, all the more smoothly will flow the dynamics of the retreat.

3. The Title and Presupposition

After the Annotations section of the book, we find a brief statement that acts as a summary description of the Exercises in terms of their purpose [21]. Ignatius desires that each person come to a fullness of freedom—the freedom of a child of God, that is, the love surrender of the crucified and risen Christ. When we put in order conflicting or competing values in our lives, we must not be at the mercy of our emotions or our prejudices if we are truly to seek and find the will of God. This kind of spiritual freedom is clearly called upon when we are faced with decisions and choices, especially those affecting our life directions.

It is also within this context of freedom that Ignatius sets the tone for the relationship between the director and the retreatant [22]. As usual, the progress or movement of the retreat itself is his major concern. Because mutual trust and openness is essential in the relationship between the director and the one being directed, Ignatius stresses how each person should be ready to give a more positive interpretation to the other's statement even if what is said or done should appear strange or even disedifying. The whole attempt to clarify, or possibly even correct, is pursued with Christian tact, understanding, and love. This principle remains the Ignatian base for all our work as Christian ministers.

4. The Foundation

Most retreatants have found that their first taste of the Exercises came in the consideration of the Principle and Foundation [23]. The Principle and Foundation had become an essential part of the Exercises by about the time of Ignatius's theology studies at the University of Paris. For Ignatius, these few brief paragraphs capture the truth about God's creation and human existence. These statements appear so basic for our relationship to God, to our fellow men and women, and to our world that we are tempted to pass over them lightly. Ignatius's own experience in giving the Exercises proves that there can be no progress or movement unless we acknowledge this base as truly our firm foundation. Before we can even begin to look at sin and our own personal rejection of God at the Ignatian level where it calls forth gratitude in us as retreatants, a basic trust in, and experience of, God's creating and sustaining love must be present. Sin itself is a faith concept and so, to realize its meaning, we need to consider first the firm foundation of our faith in our creator God as a God of all good gifts and in his creation, given as ways of coming to know and love him. Otherwise, a very unhealthy introspection and self-centered shame can become the focus of the First Week. What Ignatius intends to provoke in the retreatant is such an unflinching gaze at the aspect of sinfulness that it results in a response of thanks to a God who loves so much, both in his first creative moment and in his faithful and forgiving constancy toward his creation.

The little evidence we have of the use of the Foundation in Ignatius's time indicates that it was a brief consideration by the retreatant on the first evening or day. The deception in this evidence lies in the rather long preparation time which Ignatius himself usually presumes before a person was ready for the Exercises. Although we do not know the content of this preparatory process, it evidently enabled the retreatant to feel "at home" with this kind of summary statement about the basic biblical catechesis found in the Principle and Foundation. From this starting point, the movement or progress which is involved in the unfolding of all that lies hidden in God's salvation plan can begin. In fact, the very consideration of the way of living called for in the Foundation often rouses a sense of personal inadequacy in the retreatant's response. This inadequacy, including the sense of sinfulness, commonly introduces the movement in the retreatant towards the matter of the First Week.

5. The First Week

If we remember that Ignatius wrote down his text for use by the person who gives the Exercises, we will have a better sense for the ordering of the two pieces which form the content of the First Week. Ignatius first presents the matter when dealing with the methodology of *conscience examination* [24-43] and then describes, rather briefly, the five prayer exercises [45-71].

The process of the Ignatian retreat is predominantly a reflective one. We review or reflect upon our experiences: the prayer of the past hour, the integrating or disrupting factors affecting the retreat during this past half day, the pattern of our tendencies in our past life, and so on. An unreflective person is not an apt subject for this kind of retreat. Consequently, the director must first help a person to be reflective about his or her experiences.

When Ignatius places the method of examination first within the text, he stresses the necessary importance as well as the practical ways of being reflective for the essential progress of the retreat. The examination of conscience also has a significant place within the context of the First Week matter which deals with a person's rejection of God by sin and God's continuing response of mercy. Both the review of our own past sinfulness and the encouraged preparation for the sacrament of reconciliation [44] are facilitated by this practical introduction to examining one's conscience.

Ordinarily a temporal priority is not needed or desirable for introducing a retreatant to the process of examination before involving him in the exercises of the First Week. The movement which carries us from the Foundation consideration to the matter of the First Week calls for a simultaneous interplay between the kind of instruction involved in fostering the practical method of being reflective about oneself and the kind of direction given in prayer, as indicated in the five exercises. The director must be the one who determines how best to integrate the flow between these two pieces which form the matter of the First Week.

Ignatius makes evident in the Fourth Annotation that a *Week,* as he is using the word, does not of itself signify any set number of days. The length of time spent within each of the Four Weeks of the Exercises has to be adapted to a particular retreatant. He observes only that the total time to be spent in the Exercises is about thirty days. In light of this orientation, we can understand the rather mysterious presentation of five exercises making up five one-hour periods of prayer as the total content of the First Week's prayer time. The richness of the material outlined by Ignatius demands time for its assimilation. Even when Scripture is used to enhance the First Week's prayer, time plays an important part for absorbing the retreat experience.

The necessity of repetition allows a deepening realization to develop which produces the "intimate understanding and relish of the truth" [2] within the five prayer periods of a day in the First Week. What also becomes apparent is the dynamics of the Week; this dynamic movement is reflected in the grace sought, as expressed in the second prelude (in this First Week time) and in the colloquies indicated by Ignatius.

The first exercise [45-54] focuses on the awfulness of a single sin as revealed in the account of the angels' rejection of God, in the story of the first man and woman and their disobeying God, and in the faith understanding which we have of a person's free choice which allows him or her to reject God for all eternity. Ignatius has a retreatant look objectively at the effect of a single sin—it disrupts the whole purpose of life, rouses hatred and division, and leads to a self-enclosed death apart from the only source of life, God.

The subjective entrance of the retreatant into this exercise comes in the colloquy or intimate conversation between the retreatant and Jesus hanging on the cross concerning the consequences of a single sin [53]. Ignatius suggests that we retreatants remember that more than a single sin has touched our lives. If Jesus, our Creator and Lord (by this title Ignatius explicitly connects these reflections to the preceding Foundation consideration), takes on temporal life only to die on a cross for our sins, what can we sinners say about our own responses—in the past, even now, and in the future? The actual praying centers here in the conversation between the retreatant and Jesus (God) about various points stimulated by the matter under consideration.

This first exercise, with its three different focus points, stresses thinking and reasoning. Traditionally the method of prayer which involves this kind of thinking has been called *meditation.* This meditative style of praying forms the basic approach described by Ignatius for entering into the First Week.

The second exercise [55-61] turns the retreatant's eyes more upon his or her own story of sin. This exercise moves us from the more objective stance of our first prayer period to the more subjective stance of deep involvement in this present one. But Ignatius carefully directs the focus away from the despair due to one's faults and their effects and to the continuous support and love given by God both directly and through the gifts of nature and grace and the loving concern and support of our fellowmen and women. The colloquy aims outward from self by giving thanks to God for all the ways in which he continues to pour life into us, even as we feel the effects of our sin [61].

The third exercise [62-63] is described as a *repetition* in that it entails praying our response to the matter from the preceding two exercises. Besides interrelating the subject matter of the two preceding exercises by means of focusing on the graced insight and affect we have experienced, this third exercise makes clear that the emphasis is always on the colloquy—the subject matter being the stimulant for this conversation with God. In this exercise, Ignatius suggests that the conversation be directed to Mary, to Jesus, and to the Father.

Ignatius has two ways of inciting in the retreatant the intensity of a particular desire. Five prayer periods in a single day obviously show such an intensity. What is called the *triple colloquy* is another way. In a childlike way that makes sense only for a person of deep faith, Ignatius encourages us to line up all the help we can in terms of the grace gifts which we need. He has us go to Mary in order that she might support us with her Son, then to Jesus that he might support us before the Father, and finally to the Father to repeat again our own request. Here in this third exercise [62-63], Ignatius would have us plead for a depth of knowledge, an insight of understanding, and an ability to act against the tendencies in ourselves and in our world that lead us away from God.

The fourth exercise [64] is a time of even further refinement of the matter which is focused by our experienced insight and affect from the previous prayer period and in terms of our response through the triple colloquy. The fifth exercise [65-71] continues the same simplifying movement of prayer within the day. In the Ignatian vocabulary, this fifth period of prayer in the day is ordinarily designated as a method of praying called an "application of senses." He does not identify the fifth prayer period in the First Week by this title, although his points would seem to indicate this method of praying. A number of interpretations about the meaning and methodology of this prayer form have been proposed over the years.

From the viewpoint of dynamic movement, it is clear that the usual pattern in the retreat day is the presentation of a certain amount of material for consideration, which in successive prayer periods less and less occupies the head as the heart more and more responds in colloquy. By the time of the fifth exercise within the day, there has arisen such an easy way of being present to God within the context of the matter and our response to it that a method of praying seems difficult to describe. Truly this prayer time can be called a most passive way of praying. It is akin to the passive way that our five senses take in the data of the environment around us. In the First Week, it is a total experience of being a sinner, weighed down by our personal sin and feeling the oppression of the history of sin and its continuing presence in our world. From within this sense of immersion in sin—so complete an experience is like *hell*—we once again speak out our thanks to Christ for being so loving and merciful to us [71].

I have noted that there is a certain movement in the retreat day as described by Ignatius. In the First Week, it is a movement from thinking and reasoning to feeling—a lessening of reflection with the head and more a responding with the heart. This same kind of movement can be traced in the structures of an entire Week. In the First Week, for example, if a person were to continue to repeat the five exercises outlined by Ignatius over a three- or four-day period, each day would tend to be a bit simpler than the preceding day in terms of the matter reflected upon. What would likely grow stronger and more intense would be the emotions or affections of the retreatant when making a response.

From the direction of the dynamics present in the First Week and expressed through the prelude that requests a certain grace (what we desire) and through the colloquy (how the conversation goes between God and ourselves), it is clear that the sense of "finishing" the Week would come from the God-given peace of experiencing oneself at once as a sinner and being loved and saved as such by God. God's abiding mercy is a real experience, deeper down but just as factual as our own sinfulness. The stress which Ignatius puts on gratitude in the First Week is significant for making a judgment about a retreatant's readiness to move on to the Second Week.

6. The Second Week

The Call of Christ the King

Nowhere in the First Week does Ignatius indicate a mercy meditation with a base such as the Lucan parable of the prodigal son. Some commentators find this quite curious. But besides the fact that he has laid stress on the response of gratitude throughout the Week, itis my belief that he concretizes the mercy of God in the exercise titled the Call of the Temporal King [91-98].

There is a way of showing love by doing something for another person, as a father can send his child gifts while living afar. But a far-greater sign of love is shown by being present and being mutually involved, such as parents spending time with their children and working together at something. It is in this second way, by presence and mutual involvement, that Ignatius presents the parable of a king making an appeal to all the inhabitants of his kingdom.

The parable is intended to be a pale image—though it has been repeated many times in actual human history—of the call that Jesus Christ gives to each person. He not only identifies himself as our personal Savior but invites each man, woman, and child to be involved with him in the salvation of their fellow men and women and their world. The victory has been won in Christ, although it is still in process in us and in our world.

Ignatius would have us understand more deeply the mercy of God as it is extended by the very means of this call to work with Christ and to follow him in all the ways that our devotion to him can draw us. Ignatius proposes that we consider the response that a very generous person would make to Jesus, but he is careful not to suggest that we make the same response [97-98]. Likely it is too early in the retreat to have such generosity realistically expressed. In fact, no colloquy is outlined, although a grace has been sought in terms of hearing and responding to the call of Christ [9].

This exercise—one of the structural pieces put together by Ignatius to introduce us to the risen and present Christ and to his call as it is addressed to us here and now—is best described as a consideration. In presentation, it is more akin to the Foundation than to the exercises of the First Week. Without trying to draw too hard and fast a distinction, I note that the evident logic involved in a consideration does not demand the kind of reasoning process which the meditation form does. Both prayer forms, however, ultimately call for some response from us, eliciting our desires.

Often commentators identify the call of Christ as the "Second Foundation." As Ignatius gives the directions for this day, he indicates that this exercise should be gone through twice [99]. The common practice of the repose day or break day between the Weeks of the Exercises apparently drew its inspiration from the relaxation from the five exercises of a day in the First Week to the two exercises of this day on the Kingdom.

Although there are only two prayer-exercise periods identified for this day, since the same material about the Kingdom is repeated, the day itself is a most important one for the dynamics of the retreat. The Call of Christ is meant to rouse in the retreatant, not only a generous response of gratitude, but also a commitment to the person of Jesus and to his work. The exercise Call of the King, then, acts as a bridge between our gratitude for the mercy of God as seen in Jesus on the Cross in the First Week and our familiarizing ourselves in prayer with Jesus and his work in the succeeding Weeks. The Kingdom exercise remains also an encounter with Jesus as he is now—our risen Savior—who continues to invite each one of us to be his apostle for our own time and place.

The Contemplations

Ignatius opens up the Second Week proper with three days of exercises on the incarnation, birth, and hidden life of Jesus, respectively. The structure of each day is similar to the day described in the First Week, with new matter being presented in both the first and second exercise periods, followed by repetitions, with the final exercise being identified as an application of senses.

The grace sought (from the Second Week through the Fourth Week always expressed in the third prelude), together with the colloquy, gives us the sense of direction or movement within this Week. The grace is consistently expressed: "to know Jesus more intimately so that I can love him more and follow him more closely." The colloquies we pray tend to sharpen and shape that desire according to the particular mystery of Christ's life that provides the matter for prayer.

The way of praying found in the Second Week and in the succeeding Weeks most clearly bears the special mark of Ignatius's insight. Ignatius describes this kind of prayer as *contemplation,* and he gives to it his own special traits. His style of contemplation takes for its content various incidents (which are also called *mysteries* in Christian tradition) in the life of Christ as depicted in the Gospels. Every incident recounted in Scripture by the evangelist is matter potential for this kind of praying.

In the first and second exercise of the Second Week [101-109, 110-117], Ignatius describes two ways of approaching this kind of contemplation. The perspective of the Father, Son, and Spirit looking upon our world provides the entrance into the scene of the annunciation of the angel Gabriel to Mary. With the same total involvement as God had then, we wait for Mary's response and then rejoice to know that the Son has become man for us. For Ignatius, the idea of contemplation means to enter into the gospel scene so completely that we drink in the atmosphere, hear the nuances of what is said, and sense the meaning of gestures and actions at a depth which only a loving presence can penetrate.

The nativity of Jesus in Bethlehem is the mystery presented for the second exercise. Ignatius expands the simple Scripture setting by relating the circumstances of Jesus' birth to a comprehensive view of his life of hardship leading to death on a cross. The simple way in which Ignatius calls each retreatant to be fully present within a particular mystery of Christ's life is at the same time made more whole or integrated by his suggestions for expanding realistically one's perspectives as, for example, from the viewpoint of God or from the viewpoint of Christ's whole life leading up to his death on the cross for us.

It is by means of this style of contemplative prayer that Ignatius has discovered a way for the retreatant to imbibe Jesus' attitudes and approaches—to God, to men and women, and to his world. The more we enter into gospel contemplation, the more we heighten the connaturality of our own way of living with the way that Christ lives. By the grace we seek and by the prayer method we use, we find ourselves drinking in the experiences of Jesus, so that we begin to assimilate his values, his loves, his freedom. This style of praying provides the necessary context of Ignatian discernment or decision making, which in turn forms an essential part of the Second Week and is meant to be an abiding part of the Christian's life that is shaped by the Spiritual Exercises.

The Two Standards

On the fourth day of the Second Week, Ignatius once again outlines a structural meditation which encapsulates the identity and mission of Jesus. This meditation is called the Two Standards [136-147]; together with the Three Classes of Persons, it supplies the matter for the prayer of this particular day. The exercise of the Two Standards is to be repeated three or four times [148], so that the final prayer period is given over to the matter presented in the Three Classes of Persons.

Ignatius designedly interprets the third day of contemplations, on the hidden life of Jesus in Nazareth and the incident of his being found in the temple at the age of twelve [134], as an indication of the life direction which each person faces before God [135]. Is God's will for our life to be found in the ordinary life of a Christian as represented by Jesus' life in Nazareth, or are we called to a life of special service as hinted at in Jesus' being about his Father's business? Ignatius distills the experiences and choices made by Jesus throughout his life into the structural exercise of the Two Standards in order to help us answer that question for ourselves.

This fourth day stands out in the Second Week because the prayer is meditative and Scripture itself does not form the matter for the exercises. The grace sought is one of recognizing and understanding how the power of evil leads us further away from God and how Jesus proposes to lead us ever more surely towards himself [139]. These exercises are aimed at understanding the choice of values inherent in Christ's life—values which he wants to share with each of us.

Ignatius presents Lucifer as the personal epitome of all that is evil and inimical to human well-being. He depicts him as an apparent "angel of light" who ordinarily entices men and women to make what they own or possess the sum of their personal value or worth, and even providing them their identity. The next step that Lucifer proposes is for people to look for and demand the adulation and honor of others to give them a personal sense of worth and selfhood. Finally, there is the paradoxical enslavement within the self-conceit of pride by which we try to assert our independence from everything and everyone, including God.

Only by examining this pattern of enslavement by the power of evil do we come to some insight into the mysterious values by which Jesus lives his own life and by which we are invited to live in imitation of him. Ignatius identifies three counter steps in Jesus' choice of life values. He calls us to a poverty which will not let us measure our worth or identity by what we have or possess. He calls to a humiliation or powerlessness which will permit us to be free from the flattery or fawning behavior involved in the quest for worldly reputation and esteem. Finally, he calls to a humility that must be the ground or foundation of our lives. Just as Jesus' own identity and personal worth consist in being Son of God, so does he share that same truth with each one of us—men and women who can glory in calling upon God as Abba, Father. Why it is that we can pray for and desire poverty, humiliations, and humility becomes, by God's grace, understandable through the dynamic structuring of this meditation. But the depth of understanding that is necessary for living this choice of life values gives cause for Ignatius to employ the threefold colloquy with Mary, Jesus, and the Father in which we beg to be given such an important grace gift [147].

The Three Classes

It is not enough to understand Christ's strategy for choosing poverty, humiliations, and humility, and so for calling us to follow. We must have a readiness of will and desire to be able to follow. In order to facilitate the movement between the understanding sought in the exercise of the Two Standards and this readiness of will, Ignatius proposes the exercise entitled the Three Classes of Persons [149-156].

The exercise is simply presented as a case study of people who approach a decision in different ways. None of the persons involved actually makes a decision. But the attitudes represented by the first two groupings demonstrate a way of avoiding the kind of decision which seems to be called for. Personal preferences or attachments seem to get in the way of deciding and putting into action what is necessary. The third grouping shows by its intentions an openness and willingness to follow out whatever choice or decision God would make known to them. The third class also acknowledges the strength of certain attachments or preferences, but persons of this class do not allow themselves to be bound in or frozen where they are. They exercise their freedom to come to a decision, by God's grace, inasmuch as they are ready and available to serve God our Lord.

By means of this exercise, Ignatius has us consider and reflect upon the way people come to decisions when their affections are involved. From the objective example presented in this meditation form, he intends that we be aroused to intensify our own desire for freedom so that we express what we want by means of the threefold colloquy with Mary, with Jesus, and with the Father [156]. This final prayer exercise of the fourth day is meant to move a retreatant from the understanding of Jesus' values to a readiness for acceptance of his call in whatever way God makes it apparent in the retreatant's life.

The Three Kinds of Humility

Ignatius has one more structural piece to add at this point in the retreat. It is in the form of a consideration similar to the Principle and Foundation. The reflection deals with the many degrees of closeness to Christ, who sums up in himself the truth of what it means to be human—the humility of being Son. *Humildad*, "humility" (from the Latin *humus*, meaning *earth* or *ground*)—as Ignatius uses the word, is our foundational virtue—what truly "grounds" or provides foundation for our identity and consequently our way of living and working. In the Gospels, Jesus wants us to learn of him because he is humble: He knows where he comes from and where he is going, for he is Son, "the Beloved." That familial relationship is what Jesus has shared with us, giving us his Spirit so that we too might be one with him in calling upon God as Abba, Father. As we have been considering the value system by which Jesus lives his life, we are drawn to reflect on how closely we want to be identified with him. The uniqueness of the relationship between Jesus and each one of us indicates that there are as many kinds of humility as there are people.

Ignatius draws in broad strokes three descriptions of humility that can be found in the spectrum of close relationships [165-167]. The first kind of humility is that of a person who would do nothing to break a relationship and yet can act in ways that neither build it nor strengthen it. The second kind of humility describes a person whose whole way of living is found in his or her relationship with Jesus and his or her life orientation to do the will of the Father. This person has been pictured in the third example given in the exercise regarding the Three Classes. Ignatius goes on to outline another level of closeness, one found only in those lovers whose very external appearances and experiences seem to mesh into a unity. The person described in the third kind of humility desires so close an identity with Jesus that if the externals of his life, especially in terms of the poverty that Jesus experienced, the rejection he received, and ultimately the crucifixion he embraced, were to be mirrored in this person's life, only delight and joy would be the result. What Ignatius pictures here is the "madness" of martyrs like St. Lawrence or St. Thomas More who truly delighted in a suffering and death that, because of their love, brought them into the closest of relationships with Christ. This madness—the intoxication of love—finds its source in the grace gift of God.

After having the retreatant consider over some period of time these notions about intimacy in following Jesus, Ignatius suggests that the retreatant might pray to be given the grace of this third kind of intimacy with Jesus, if it would be God's will and if it would give God greater glory [168]. The intensity of the request should be reflected in the threefold colloquy with Mary, with Jesus, and with the Father.

It is clear that in these three structural pieces—the Two Standards, the Three Classes, and the Three Kinds of Humility—Ignatius has strongly prepared the retreatant for the contemplations concerning the following of Jesus in his public life. We as retreatants have achieved an understanding of Christ's identity and values, a readiness and willingness to follow, and a deep desire for the grace to be admitted to such a close intimacy with Christ that, if possible, even the externals of his life might be reflected in our own.

The Public Life of Jesus

With this kind of heightened interior state, the retreatant enters into the contemplations of Jesus' public life, beginning with his baptism by John at the river Jordan, the temptations in the desert, the call of the apostles, and so on. Once again, because of differences among retreatants, their desires, and the ways in which God works with them, directors will vary their use of the Scripture passages suggested for the content of this Week.

Two aspects of the Ignatian approach, however, should be noted. The mysteries of Christ's public life which are chosen by Ignatius are *ordered* in terms of the direction of the retreat. The selection of passages is not based on the simple chronological sequence within a given Gospel or on a random choice of a director's or a retreatant's favorite gospel incidents. Rather, the mysteries chosen are always ordered to the progress of this particular retreatant's response to the lead of God. In addition, Ignatius is not a man who thinks that the more passages suggested by the director and the more covered by the retreatant, the better. Rather, just the opposite is indicated by the directions which Ignatius himself gives. In view of the importance of this retreat for the desired orientation of the retreatant's life, Ignatius suggests only one scriptural passage a day [159], with either three or four repetitions of the same matter. A central purpose of the contemplations is to allow a retreatant to live so closely with Jesus that there is more an immersion into his very person than there is an accumulation of knowledge about Scripture passages, which might come from examining even more passages. The Ignatian dynamics inherent in the contemplations consists in fostering a depth in the relationship which will give relish to the companionship with Jesus and the following of Jesus that we are seeking in the retreat.

The Election

The structural pieces of the fourth day in the Second Week clearly mark the natural flow towards the making of practical decisions about our lives in relationship to our following of Jesus. It is obvious from the placement of the material on election in the text of the Second Week, as well as from the historical evidence of Ignatius's conduct in giving the Exercises, that the choice of a state of life or the reformation of life is a central aspect of the retreat [169-189].

But as we see in the Third Class of Persons and in the Third Degree of Humility, Ignatius provides a far broader purpose in making the retreat, one that subsumes any particular decision or reform of life. By means of the contemplations, he expects a certain connaturality to develop in us such that the way in which Jesus responds to his Father, to his fellow men and women, and to his life's events becomes more and more our way of response. It is only when this atmosphere is nurtured that the Ignatian process of discernment can properly be realized. For him, the way to live life and to make life's decisions in accord with the will of God is not through a process of reasoning, or even of praying, about our decisions. It is through the continuing process of "putting on the mind of Christ Jesus"—a process brought about by our focusing on Jesus through contemplation.

7. The Third Week

The sense of some resolution about the Third Kind of Humility or about a life decision provides the usual indication that the time has come to move on to the Third Week. In general, this movement is subtler and more gently concluded than the flow between the First and the Second Weeks.

Contemplation remains the style of prayer. Ignatius introduces a special nuance through the identification of six points rather than the three points common to the Second Week exercises. All three added points [195-197] focus upon a greater interiority in the approach to whatever mystery of Jesus' life is under consideration. These added focal points are supplemented by Ignatius's review of the meaning and method of the colloquy, in which the stress is now not so much on the familiarity of conversation as on the intimacy of the affect of compassion [199].

By means of these different emphases, along with the grace sought in the Third Week exercises, we are made aware that there is a stress now, not so much in terms of the activity of following Jesus, but more in view of a "staying with" him in his passion and death. To be able to enter into his sorrow and to go deeper than the observation of exterior pain to the inner suffering of Jesus expresses the grace asked for in this Week [193]. We ask that Jesus would share with us how he experienced his passion. One other element which Ignatius underlines for this passion time is the notion of "all this for me." He is most concerned that the redemptive act of Jesus not be drawn in cosmic terms, to the detriment of the unique and personal love for this particular retreatant that moves Jesus to spend his life even for this one person in the face of his or her sin rejection.

The intensity of the Week comes out in the five prayer periods and in the suggestion that the triple colloquy with Mary, with Jesus, and with the Father might be the common practice throughout the Week. There is a greater freedom of approach used in this Week, even to the suggestion that whole days be spent on the total account of the passion rather than on its individual mysteries [209]. Whatever seems best in view of the particular retreatant receives an increasingly greater emphasis as the retreat progresses.

At the conclusion of the text of the Third Week, we find the *reglas* or guidelines for eating [210-217]. Although there may be legitimate speculation as to exactly how these guidelines or norms are to be integrated into the overall dynamics of the retreat, it seems foolish to deny that Ignatius took as much care to place these guidelines at this juncture of the retreat as he did with all the other structural pieces. By their very title in the text (*Reglas . . . para Adelante*) [210], these guidelines look to the future—the Fourth Week and thereafter. They present a practical pattern for developing the means to live as Jesus lives, as applied to the most common and everyday experience—eating.

Ignatius gives us here a model of practically carrying out our following of Christ throughout the totality of our day. He begins the process by having us consider the means which we must use in our ordinary lives to continue to live as closely with Christ as Christ has drawn us to do in this retreat. In the context of the remaining days of the retreat, there are some things we can begin to do even now, which look to our awareness of the present and risen Christ and the ways in which he makes himself present in our world. The guidelines for eating, then, are a consideration providing a kind of bridge over to our following of the contemporary Christ of the Fourth Week.

8. The Fourth Week

The Fourth Week of the Exercises deals with the risen life of Jesus. Contemplation remains the style of the prayer exercises. Although Ignatius continues to call for the freedom of approach used in the Third Week for adapting the movement to a particular retreatant, this is the only Week in which he does not encourage five periods of prayer and repetitions. Instead, he presumes a new mystery is to be used for each of the first three periods of prayer, with the application of senses remaining the method for the summation of the prayer experiences of the day [227].

The emphasis in these contemplations is not so much on the persons with whom Jesus deals or the activities he does as it is on the consistency of Jesus in his risen life—in his desire to dispel fear, to give his peace, and to send us out with the Good News. The risen Jesus stands forth as one who consoles and strengthens.

The grace sought and the colloquy proposed again give us clues to the direction of this Week. We pray for the grace to enter into the joy of our risen Lord—the one who has broken the chains of death, has defeated the power of sin and evil, and is the firstborn of the new creation [221]. The compassion with which we could labor with Jesus in his suffering and death is now changed over into the joy we share in his victory, even though we ourselves still experience the struggle towards the fullness of that new life. From our contemplations of the risen Christ dealing with frightened men and women so like us, we gradually come to appreciate that we ourselves and our world have been radically changed by Jesus' resurrection.

It is in this light that we better understand the exercise entitled the Contemplation on the Love of God [230-237]. The movement, seen in the grace desired together with the colloquy, returns once again to the notion of gratitude to a loving God—a gratitude that empowers us to live a life of service in following Our Lord and God [233]. There is a certain review of the overall dynamics of the Four Weeks of the Exercises as present here in the four focal points of this exercise. Because this material is not new, it does not require a reasoning process, and the prayer period can truly be a contemplative way of praying.

Each of the four points continues the particular dynamics found in the Gospel contemplations of this Week. Just as the Lord's activity is to console and share his joy with his mother and disciples, so too he continues that effort with us today. Ignatius focuses that consoling activity of our Lord and God in terms of his gifts of nature and grace to us, the gift of his irrevocable identity with us, the gift of his continuing compassion for us in our labors and struggles, and the permeating flow of his life all around us in this new creation.

In Ignatius's own prenote to this exercise [230-231], he has made clear his understanding of lovers as being people who want to share mutually whatever knowledge, feelings, abilities, and so on that they have. His Spanish words *comunicacion* and *comunicar* suggest how true love is always a communicating love. The original Ignatian prayer response which forms the suggested colloquy—the *Suscipe* or "Take and Receive"—communicates our own sense of embodying our gift of self to God. As God has shared his life with us, so we desire and ask him to receive the sharing of our whole life with him.

This gentle expression of our love marks the continuing dynamics of a life now permanently affected by the Spiritual Exercises of St. Ignatius:

Take, Lord, and receive
all my liberty, my memory, my understanding,
and my entire will—
all that I have and call my own.
You have given it all to me.
To you, Lord, I return it.
Everything is yours.
Do with it what you will.
Give me only your love and your grace.
That is enough for me.

Appendix Two

THE PRAYER "SOUL OF CHRIST"

Tradition has it that Ignatius Loyola had great affection for the *Anima Christi* ("Soul of Christ") prayer. I believe that he found delight in this prayer because it summed up in its own devotional way the dynamics present in the Exercises: "I live, now no longer I, but Christ lives in me."

Traditional Translation	Contemporary "Reading"
Soul of Christ, sanctify me.	Jesus, may all that is you flow into me.
Body of Christ, save me.	May your body and blood be my food and drink.
Blood of Christ, inebriate me.	May your passion and death be my strength
Water from the side of Christ, wash me.	and life.
Passion of Christ, strengthen me.	Jesus, with you by my side enough has
O good Jesus, hear me.	been given.
Within thy wounds hide me	May the shelter I seek be the shadow of
And permit me not to be separated	your cross.
from thee.	Let me not run from the love which you offer,
From the wicked enemy defend me.	But hold me safe from the forces of evil.
In the hour of my death call me,	On each of my dyings shed your light and
And bid me come to thee	your love.
That with thy saints I may praise thee	Keep calling to me until that day comes
Forever and ever.	When, with your saints, I may praise you forever.
Amen.	Amen.

A SELECT BIBLIOGRAPHY OF READINGS IN ENGLISH ON THE SPIRITUAL EXERCISES OF ST. IGNATIUS LOYOLA

The Text of the Exercises

Fleming, David L., SJ. *Draw Me into Your Friendship: A Literal Translation and a Contemporary Reading of the Spiritual Exercises*. St. Louis: Institute of Jesuit Sources, 1996.

Ganss, George E., SJ. *The Spiritual Exercises of Saint Ignatius: A Translation and Commentary*. St. Louis: Institute of Jesuit Sources, 1992.

Puhl, Louis J., SJ. *The Spiritual Exercises of St. Ignatius: A New Translation Based on Studies in the Language of the Autograph*. Chicago: Loyola Press, 1968. First published 1951 by Newman Press.

Tetlow, Joseph A., SJ. *Choosing Christ in the World: A Handbook for Directing the Spiritual Exercises of St. Ignatius Loyola according to Annotations Eighteen and Nineteen*. Rev. ed. St. Louis: Institute of Jesuit Sources, 1999.

———. *Ignatius Loyola: Spiritual Exercises*. New York: Crossroad, 1992.

———. *Lightworks: Some Simple Exercises according to Annotation Eighteen of the Spiritual Exercises*. St. Louis: Institute of Jesuit Sources, 1999. Also published as an appendix to the author's *Choosing Christ in the World*, 1999 (above).

The Context of the Exercises

Barry, William A., SJ. *Finding God in All Things: A Companion to the Spiritual Exercises of St. Ignatius*. Notre Dame: Ave Maria Press, 1991.

———. *Letting God Come Close: An Approach to the Ignatian Spiritual Exercises*. Chicago: Loyola Press, 2001.

Begheyn, Paul, SJ, and Kenneth Bogart, SJ. "A Bibliography on St. Ignatius's *Spiritual Exercises*," *Studies in the Spirituality of Jesuits* 23, no. 3 (May 1991).

Coathalem, Hervé, SJ. *Ignatian Insights: A Guide to the Complete Spiritual Exercises*. Trans. Charles J. McCarthy, SJ. 2nd ed. Taichung, Taiwan: Kuangchi Press, 1971.

Dister, John E., SJ, ed. *A New Introduction to the Spiritual Exercises of St. Ignatius*. Eugene, Oreg.: Wipf and Stock, 2003. First published 1994 by Liturgical Press.

Ivens, Michael, SJ. *Understanding the Spiritual Exercises: Text and Commentary; A Handbook for Retreat Directors*. Leominster, U.K.: Gracewing, 1998.

Lonsdale, David, SJ. *Eyes to See, Ears to Hear: An Introduction to Ignatian Spirituality*. Chicago: Loyola Press, 1991. Reprint, Maryknoll, N.Y.: Orbis Books, 2000.

Palmer, Martin E., SJ, ed. and trans. *On Giving the Spiritual Exercises: The Early Jesuit Manuscript Directories and the Official Directory of 1599*. St. Louis: Institute of Jesuit Sources, 1996.

Peters, William A. M., SJ. *The Spiritual Exercises of St. Ignatius: Exposition and Interpretation*. 2nd ed. Rome: Centrum Ignatianum Spiritualitatis, 1978.

Commentary/Readings on the Text

Fleming, David L., SJ. *Notes on the Spiritual Exercises*. 2nd ed. St. Louis: Review for Religious, 1983.

———. *Ignatian Exercises: Contemporary Annotations*. St. Louis: Review for Religious, 1996.

Sheldrake, Philip, SJ, ed. *The Way of Ignatius Loyola: Contemporary Approaches to the Spiritual Exercises*. St. Louis: Institute of Jesuit Sources, 1991.

General Ignatian Readings

Becker, Kenneth L. *Unlikely Companions: C. G. Jung on the Spiritual Exercises of Ignatius of Loyola; An Exposition and Critique Based on Jung's Lectures and Writings*. Foreword by Karl Rahner, SJ. London: Gracewing, 2002.

Cowan, Marian, CSJ, and John Carroll Futrell, SJ. *Companions in Grace: A Handbook for Directors of the Spiritual Exercises of St. Ignatius of*

Loyola. St. Louis: Institute of Jesuit Sources, 2000. First published 1982 by Le Jacq.

Cusson, Gilles, SJ. *Biblical Theology and the Spiritual Exercises: A Method and a Biblical Interpretation*. Trans. Mary A. Roduit, RC, and George E. Ganss, SJ. St. Louis: Institute of Jesuit Sources, 1988.

Divarkar, Parmananda R., SJ, trans. *A Pilgrim's Testament: The Memoirs of Ignatius of Loyola as Transcribed by Luís Gonçalves da Câmara*. St. Louis: Institute of Jesuit Sources, 1995.

Du Brul, Peter, SJ. *Ignatius: Sharing the Pilgrim Story; A Reading of the Autobiography of St. Ignatius of Loyola*. Leominster, U.K.: Gracewing, 2003.

Dyckman, Katherine, SNJM, Mary Garvin, SNJM, and Elizabeth Liebert, SNJM. *The Spiritual Exercises Reclaimed: Uncovering Liberating Possibilities for Women*. Mahwah, N.J.: Paulist Press, 2001.

Egan, Harvey D., SJ. *The Spiritual Exercises and the Ignatian Mystical Horizon*. St. Louis: Institute of Jesuit Sources, 1976.

Endean, Philip, SJ. *Karl Rahner and Ignatian Spirituality*. Oxford University Press, 2001.

English, John J., SJ. *Spiritual Freedom: From an Experience of the Ignatian Exercises to the Art of Spiritual Guidance*. 2nd ed. Chicago: Loyola Press, 1995.

Ganss, George E., SJ, ed. *Ignatius of Loyola: The Spiritual Exercises and Selected Works*. Mahwah, N.J.: Paulist Press, 1991.

Nicolás, Antonio T. de. *Powers of Imagining: Ignatius de Loyola; A Philosophical Hermeneutic of Imaging through the Collected Works of Ignatius de Loyola with a Translation of These Works*. Albany: State University of New York Press, 1986.

Olin, John C., ed., and John F. O'Callaghan, SJ, trans. *The Autobiography of St. Ignatius Loyola, with Related Documents*. New York: Fordham University Press, 1993. First published 1974 by Harper and Row.

Rahner, Hugo, SJ. *Ignatius the Theologian*. Trans. Michael Barry, SJ. San Francisco: Ignatius Press, 1991. First published 1968 by Herder and Herder.

———. *The Spirituality of St. Ignatius Loyola: An Account of Its Historical Development*. Trans. Francis John Smith, SJ. Chicago: Loyola University Press, 1968. First published 1953 by Newman Press.

Schner, George P., SJ, ed. *Ignatian Spirituality in a Secular Age*. Waterloo, Ontario: Wilfrid Laurier University Press, 1984.

Tylenda, Jospeh N., SJ, ed. *A Pilgrim's Journey: The Autobiography of Ignatius of Loyola; Introduction, Translation and Commentary*. Rev. ed. San Francisco: Ignatius Press, 2001.

Yeomans, William. *Inigo: Original Testament: The Autobiography of St. Ignatius Loyola*. London: Inigo International Centre, 1985.

Young, William J., SJ, trans. *St. Ignatius's Own Story as Told to Luis González de Cámara, with a Sampling of His Letters*. Chicago: Loyola University Press, 1982. First published 1956 by Regnery.

The Nineteenth Annotation

Cusson, Gilles, SJ. *The Spiritual Exercises Made in Everyday Life: A Method and a Biblical Interpretation*. Trans. Mary Angela Roduit, RC, and George E. Ganss, SJ. St. Louis: Institute of Jesuit Sources, 1989.

O'Hara, Tom. *At Home with the Spirit: On Retreat in Daily Life*. Mahwah, N.J.: Paulist Press, 1992.

Skehan, James W., SJ. *Director's Guide to Place Me With Your Son: Ignatian Spirituality in Everyday Life*. 3rd ed. Washington, D.C.: Georgetown University Press, 1994.

————. *Place Me With Your Son: Ignatian Spirituality in Everyday Life; Guidelines for Those Who Direct the Spiritual Exercises Arranged as a 24-Week Retreat in 4 Phases According to the 19th Annotation*. 3rd ed. Washington, DC: Georgetown University Press, 1991.

Smith, Carol Ann, SHCJ, and Eugene Merz, SJ. *Moment by Moment: A Retreat in Everyday Life*. Notre Dame: Ave Maria Press, 2000.

Veltri, John A., SJ. *Orientations*. Vol. 1, *A Collection of Helps for Meditation and Prayer*. Rev. ed. Guelph, Ontario: Loyola House, 1993. Distributed by B. Broughton, Toronto. Also available online at http://www.sentex.net/~jveltri/bob/veltri.htm.

————. *Orientations*. Vol. 2 *(Part A and Part B), For Those Who Accompany Others on the Inward Journey*. [Exp. ed.] Guelph, Ontario: Loyola House, 1998. Distributed by B. Broughton, Toronto. Also available online at http://www.sentex.net/~bjmitch/veltri.html. First, "tentative" edition published 1981 as *Orientations*. Vol. 2, *A Manual to Aid Beginning Directors of the Spiritual Exercises according to Annotation 19*.

Discernment

Lonsdale, David, SJ. *Listening to the Music of the Spirit.* Notre Dame: Ave
    Maria Press, 1993. First published 1992 in London.

Toner, Jules J., SJ. *A Commentary on Saint Ignatius's Rules for the
    Discernment of Spirits: A Guide to the Principles and Practice.* St.
    Louis: Institute of Jesuit Sources, 1982.

————. *Discerning God's Will: Ignatius of Loyola's Teaching on Christian
    Decision Making.* St. Louis: Institute of Jesuit Sources, 1991.

————. *Spirit of Light or Darkness? A Casebook for Studying Discernment
    of Spirits.* St. Louis: Institute of Jesuit Sources, 1995.

————. What Is Your Will, O God? A Casebook for Studying Discernment
    of God's Will. St. Louis: Institute of Jesuit Sources, 1995.